To Jenny,
God keeps pouring His love
through you, and that love
keeps healing me.

LOVE STYLES

why you love the way you do (and how to change it)

kevin a. thompson

thrive

Love Styles

©2025 by Kevin A. Thompson

Published by: Thrive Media

Designed by: Dave Eaton

ISBN: 979-8-9880791-5-6

Printed in the United States of America

TABLE OF CONTENTS

INTRODUCTION

As we drove through the foothills of the Sierra Nevada following a Mother's Day celebration, my mom broke the silence by asking, "What have you been reading lately?"

Our shared love for information, ideas, and books is always an easy conversation starter. That's when I told her about Attachment Theory. After sharing the concepts, I mentioned it's not unusual for one person with a primarily anxious pattern and another with a primarily avoidant pattern to be attracted to each other. But, left unaware of their tendencies, they can often struggle and not know why. "Like your father and me?" she inquired.

Almost three decades removed from their second divorce, my parents never discussed their marriages with me. Out of respect for each other and my sister and me, they held healthy/strong boundaries. But in this vulnerable moment, my mom asked a fair question about this new concept.

"Yes," I responded. "The two of you likely had no chance. You didn't know. Counselors didn't know. Today, there is something you both could have done about it, but back then, you likely had no chance."

We rode a bit more in silence, each embracing a truth that had not always been felt or understood—sometimes things don't work out despite the best of intentions. Sometimes our greatest sorrows aren't necessarily the result of a villain, but are the results of broken people just trying to figure out life in a broken world.

And sometimes, we struggle to love well, not because of evil hearts, but because of old wiring.

HIDDEN THERMOSTATS

Every couple brings something into marriage. Jason and Emily brought paintbrushes, Pinterest boards, and a hidden problem.

Newly engaged, Jason and Emily bought their first house before saying, "I do." It needed major renovations, and the couple thought the upgrades would take about as much time as their engagement. While their friends thought they were crazy, Jason and Emily believed taking on the project would be an effective transition to marriage, forcing them to talk, listen, and learn to work together under pressure.

Part of the renovation involved relocating the upstairs thermostat. Jason pulled the face off the old one, which didn't seem to work well, but he forgot to unwire the hardware. During all the other upgrades, he dry walled over the old, but still working, thermostat.

Neither Jason nor Emily realized they had never replaced the thermostat.

The renovation was complete just in time for the couple to exchange vows. After a summer honeymoon, they moved into their new home. But as fall turned to winter, they began to feel discomfort.

Their bedroom was never the desired temperature. Some nights were stiflingly hot, while others were weirdly cold. No matter what they did—more blankets, a space heater, a ceiling fan...they couldn't get the temperature right.

What they didn't know was that the original thermostat was still connected. And it was still trying to regulate the room. Hidden behind a wall and unable to sense the real environment, it was responding to a climate it couldn't actually sense. So, the temperature was constantly off. Not dramatically, just enough to make them feel consistently uncomfortable.

The same thing was happening in their marriage.

Jason and Emily hadn't just brought new paint, wallpaper, and a different floor plan into the new home. They also brought separate attachment systems: those invisible, internal thermostats that had been forming since childhood.

Jason's thermostat was wired for independence. Growing up, emotions weren't really discussed in his home. When things got tense, the unspoken rule was, "don't rock the boat". So, now, when conflict arose in marriage, his inner thermostat reacted by shutting down. He would try to cool the room, even when it needed warmth and conversation.

Emily's thermostat was wired for closeness. Her parents had been affectionate, but their behavior was unpredictable. So, she learned to stay emotionally alert, always tuning in, always trying to draw a connection before it slipped away. She would try to warm the room, even when it needed separation and differentiation.

Now, in marriage, their wiring clashed. Jason sought independence. Emily chased a connection. Both misread what the moment needed.

Not only were the thermostats struggling against each other, but they were also hidden from view. Neither Jason nor Emily understood what was going on. All they knew was that marriage was more complicated than they expected.

They both regularly felt confused, uncomfortable, and misunderstood. They didn't know why.

The issue was attachment.

Attachment is like that hidden thermostat. It's always on. Always working. Always shaping the emotional climate of a relationship.

But most of us don't know it's there. We don't understand how it works. The result is our relationships often feel beyond our control. While we desire meaningful connections, our actions usually lead to outcomes that are the exact opposite of our intentions. We try to fix the symptoms—more communication, more dates, more sex, more effort—but no matter what we do, the climate feels off.

Most people don't think about attachment; however, it shapes how you love, how you fight, how you run away, and how you come back. It's the invisible system behind every relationship you've ever had, especially the most intimate relationships.

Attachment is unseen, but it's always working and constantly shaping the emotional climate of our relationships.

But once you name it, you can change it. And that's what this book is about.

WHY ATTACHMENT ISN'T JUST PSYCHOLOGY

I'm not a psychologist. I'm a pastor.

Yet as I sat in both psychology and theology classes while in graduate school, I kept seeing a connection between what my psychology professors described as attachment and what my theology professors described as the relational fallout of human sin. Secure attachment sure sounded like Genesis 2, and non-secure attachment sounded like Genesis 3 and beyond.

After 20 years of walking with people through the highs and lows of marriage, parenting, and faith, I can tell you this: most of what we call "relational issues" are actually attachment issues in disguise.

It's why couples who truly love each other just can't stop

fighting. It's why parents feel disconnected from their kids, but they don't know why. It's why some struggle to trust God, connect with the Church, or have a compassionate understanding of the brokenness of the world.

Attachment theory, while rooted in psychology, tells a deeply biblical story. It explains what went wrong in Genesis 3 – how fear and shame replaced safety and connection. It shows how sin rewires our relational instincts and how redemption calls us to relearn what it means to love and be loved.

God created us for secure love. Jesus modeled it. The gospel makes it possible again.

That's why I'm writing this book: not as an expert with all the answers, but as a fellow traveler who has benefited from a journey of discovery and who wants to introduce you to a similar path. Just gaining some understanding can be a gift, freeing us to discover why some past relationships haven't worked. But the hope of this book is greater than just understanding; it's change. While our pasts greatly influence how we presently love, we are not imprisoned by our current patterns and behaviors. Insight can lead to understanding, which can lead to change.

My prayer is that this book gives you language for what you've felt, hope for what could be, and tools to help you love more like Jesus.

CHAPTER 1:

WHAT IS ATTACHMENT THEORY?

How our individual needs were met (or unmet) in the first few years of life forms a blueprint for how we view ourselves, others, and God. This is the basic premise of Attachment Theory. It explains why some people pursue connection, others pull away, and many bounce between the two.

The theory was proposed in the late 1950s by British psychiatrist John Bowlby. Like many upper-class British children of his time, Bowlby was largely raised by a nanny and sent away to boarding school at a young age. Experiencing both physical and emotional distance from his parents, he later wondered: What happens to children when they are separated from those they love?[1]

While Sigmund Freud greatly influenced the psychological thinking of Bowlby's day, he disagreed with the Freudian thought that children bond with their caregivers primarily because they provide food and basic needs. Instead, Bowlby believed there was an ingrained need for emotional closeness and safety.

Following World War II, Bowlby worked with children dislocated from their homes and separated from their families. He noticed these children didn't just *miss* their parents. Some became withdrawn, others clingy, some angry, and others distant. Many struggled with intimate relationships later in life. This led Bowlby to propose that emotional connection is a basic human need.

In the same way animals are born with survival instincts, Bowlby believed human babies are born with a need to connect and an instinct to do so through crying, clinging, watching, and following caregivers. While others believed these were learned behaviors, Bowlby believed they were instinctual strategies meant to protect a child.

He proposed that a child's "attachment" to their primary caregiver creates a secure base. This attachment helps the child feel safe enough to explore the world, knowing they can return to the caregiver for comfort and support. When this bond is healthy, the child learns to trust others, value themselves, and handle life's challenges. But if the bond is inconsistent or broken, it can lead to fear, anxiety, and uncertainty in oneself and others. Ultimately, the attachment shapes future relationships.

In studying 45 juvenile thieves, Bowlby discovered many had experienced early separation or loss. He concluded a lack of secure attachment could lead to severe emotional problems.

Working alongside Bowlby during these formative years was psychologist Mary Ainsworth. Having contributed to his early work in the 1950s, Ainsworth moved to Uganda in the 1960s. It was there she noticed patterns in how children sought comfort and how mothers responded. Some children seemed secure and confident in their caregivers' presence, while others were anxious or withdrawn.

This led Ainsworth to develop the Infant Strange Situation, a groundbreaking experiment that allowed psychologists to study how children responded to short separations and reunions with caregivers.

THE INFANT STRANGE SITUATION

Ainsworth's observational study consists of several short episodes (each lasting 2-3 minutes) in which a small child experiences separations and reunions with the caregiver and interactions with a stranger.

A child and their caregiver are brought into a playroom where an adult chair is present, and a chair for the child is very near the adult chair. Across the room is an area with toys. The caregiver is instructed to sit in the chair as the observer leaves the room. Then the episodes begin:

1. The parent and child are alone in the room.
2. A stranger enters the room and slowly interacts with the child.
3. The parent quietly leaves the room, leaving the child with the stranger.

4. The parent returns, and the stranger leaves.
5. The parent leaves, and the child is alone.
6. The stranger returns and tries to comfort the child.
7. The parent returns and the stranger leaves.

During each episode, observers pay close attention to how the toddler behaves, especially how they respond to stress and whether or not they seek comfort and reassurance.

Consider what we would expect to see in a normal situation for a child to go through each of these episodes.

1. Parent and child enter the room: The child sees the adult is comfortable and, after some time, begins to explore the room while looking back and checking in with the parent to make sure everything is okay.

2. Stranger enters and interacts: the child is wary of the stranger, but notices the calmness of their caregiver and isn't overly alarmed. The child watches the stranger but stays close to the caregiver.

3. Parent leaves, stranger stays: the child becomes distressed. They may cry or reach for the door. May seek some comfort from the stranger, but may also remain leery.

4. Parent returns, stranger leaves: the child quickly seeks comfort from the parent and is soothed. Eventually returns to play with the toys.

5. Parent leaves, child is alone: The child is clearly distressed. They may cry and they clearly show awareness and distress of parent's absence.

6. Stranger returns: The child remains. She may seek minimal comfort from the stranger but still prefers the parent.

7. Parent returns: The child seeks comfort from the parent, is quickly soothed, and returns to exploring the room.

While different temperaments may affect a specific child's response, we would expect most children to respond similarly, given the situation. And in

Ainsworth's experiment, many children did respond exactly as one would expect. Ultimately, this response became known as characteristic of a secure attachment.

In a secure attachment, the child uses their caregiver as a gauge to judge new situations and people. They are the thermostat for the child, helping the child understand when situations are dangerous or safe and whether other people are to be feared or trusted. The child uses the parent to regulate themselves in times of uncertainty.

While many responded this way, Ainsworth noticed not all children did. Instead, some had peculiar behavior.

1. **Parent and child enter the room:** Some children were reluctant to explore while others were quick to run to the toys with little thought of the parent.

2. **Stranger enters and interacts:** Some children were instantly upset and ran to the parent, but others were unmoved by the new person.

3. Parent leaves, stranger stays: Some children became instantly upset and not easily comforted, possibly running to the stranger but also pulling away, while other children weren't that distressed by their parent's absence and just kept playing.

4. Parent returns, the stranger leaves: Some children quickly ran to their parent but were not easily comforted. Other children ignored the parent.

5. Parent leaves, and the child is alone: Some children were overwhelmed, showing significant distress while other children showed little outward distress to the parent's absence.

6. Stranger returns: Some children continued being overwhelmed, unable to get any comfort from the stranger while others seemed unmoved by the return of the stranger.

7. Parent returns: Some children approached the parent but resisted being picked up. They seemed angry, clingy, or inconsolable, while other children were unmoved by the parent's presence. They were neither overtly distressed nor did they seek physical comfort.

Each of these responses was different from what one would expect in a typical situation. They were less healthy responses than the ideal. They are the characteristics of non-secure attachments.

Within the non-secure category, Ainsworth distinguished two contrasting responses—anxious and avoidant. For many years, the three categories of attachment were secure, anxious, and avoidant. Two decades later, Mary Main and others identified a third type of non-secure attachment, calling it disorganized attachment.[2]

TWO PATHWAYS:
SECURE AND NON-SECURE ATTACHMENT

Too often, people approach attachment theory like a personality quiz, trying to pin down their exact style—secure, anxious, avoidant, or disorganized. While these categories are helpful and we will identify with some more than others, we should be hesitant to find our "type". That language becomes too restrictive, and possibly self-fulfilling.

When Amber discovered attachment theory, it was liberating. Her online assessment didn't make much sense to her, but reading a popular book on attachment seemed to explain her whole life. Suddenly everything made sense—why she texted repeatedly when someone didn't respond to her, why silence felt like rejection, why she always apologized to people even when something wasn't her fault. "I'm anxiously attached," she proudly told her friends, relieved to finally have some understanding for her inner chaos.

But over time, nothing changed. In conflict, she would dismiss her overreactions as just what she did. When she felt triggered, she would explain her emotional spiral was just her anxious attachment. Rather than using insight to grow, she used it as an excuse for poor behavior.

Her *type* became her definition, and there was nothing she could do about it. The more she read about attachment, the more she began incorporating additional anxious attachment approaches because she assumed the label defined who she was. Anxious wasn't how she occasionally acted; it's who she was. It became a self-fulfilling prophecy.

Yet that's not the point of Attachment Theory. It's not a definition of who we are; it's an explanation of patterns of behavior and a pathway toward growth.

This is why our primary description shouldn't be anxious, avoidant, or disorganized. Instead, we should see behavior as either secure or non-secure. We will break down non-secure behavior into subcategories to better understand what we are doing and make better choices, but distinguishing between anxious or avoidant will not assist in our relationships. Instead, recognizing non-secure actions and choosing a secure pathway will be the road toward healing.

While Stan Tatkin *(Wired for Love)* writes about anchors, islands, and waves and Amir Levine *(Attached)* writes about types, Dan Siegel, founder of Interpersonal Neurobiology and psychologist at UCLA, prefers different language: patterns and pathways.

Rather than seeing attachment as fixed categories, Siegel describes them as pathways, ways of being shaped by early experience, but not hardwired into our identity.

This viewpoint places choice and change at the center of ourselves and our relationships. It demonstrates our freedom and ability to make healthier choices and to adopt new habits.

Thinking in terms of secure versus non-secure allows us to focus on what truly matters: how we respond to closeness, manage stress and separation, and repair disconnection. It reminds us that the answer to non-secure patterns is not the opposite non-secure pattern but a secure approach. It simplifies the goal. We don't have to determine what label best fits us; we simply need to learn what a secure approach is and how to make a secure pathway our go-to behavior.

ATTACHMENT STYLE	BEHAVIOR IN RELATIONSHIPS	ROOT BELIEF
Secure	Can give and receive love, manage conflict, and seek comfort when needed	"I'm safe with or without you."
Anxious	Clings, fears abandonment, craves reassurance	"You'll leave me."
Avoidant	Withdraws, values independence, avoids emotion	"You'll smother me."
Disorganized	Push-pull, unpredictable, often tied to trauma	"You'll hurt me."

THE TWO MOST COMMON OBJECTIONS

When people first hear about Attachment Theory, two primary objections arise. Ironically, they are tied to non-secure attachment. Those with anxious tendencies often worry, "Am I just blaming my parents?" While those with avoidant patterns might shrug, "The past is in the past, why dig it up?" Both objections are fair, but neither is the intent of Attachment Theory.

EMPATHY, NOT JUDGMENT; EMPOWERMENT, NOT EXCUSES

Attachment Theory puts a major emphasis on our primary caregivers, but the intention is not to shift blame for our lives from us and to our parents. At its core, attachment theory is not about blame or escape. It's about understanding. It offers a framework to help us make sense of our emotional world, relational patterns, and the assumptions we've developed to help us feel safe, seen, and secure.

Our primary caregivers played a vital role in shaping how we relate to ourselves, others, and God, but that doesn't mean they were malicious or neglectful. Most were doing the best with what they had. It means that they had their own attachment wounds as well and understanding our story can lead to empathy for their story. A simple test for whether we have truly done the work regarding how we became us, is whether we look at our

What saved you in the past might kill you in the present.

primary caregivers with more empathy or less. The better we understand Attachment Theory, the more empathy we have for others, including our parents.

While it's true some caregivers make horrific, abusive decisions, many relate more to my story—two parents who deeply loved me and would never do anything to harm me. Yet, I did not grow up with a secure attachment. This wasn't the byproduct of the absence of love; it was the result of various circumstances. For many, non-secure attachment isn't the result of their parents failing to love them, but rather a lack of skill or understanding on the part of the parents, their own attachment wounds, and life circumstances that prevented their needs from being met.

Most parents did the best they could with the tools, understanding, and awareness available to them at the time. Attachment Theory doesn't require us to vilify them. Instead, it invites us to recognize our patterns were adaptive responses to the environment in which we were raised. These patterns helped us survive emotionally. But what helped us survive then might be holding us back now.

Consider my son. Is it possible he regularly had needs that went unmet? Yes. These were not the result of Jenny or me failing to love him. We loved him to the maximum amount that love can be given. Yet in his first few years of life, he lost a grandfather to an aggressive cancer and two great-grandparents who lived next door to us. As much as we loved him, did we overlook some of his needs even as we were navigating these illnesses and deaths?

Most of our attachment wounds are not about a failure of heart, but a lack of skill.

Those unexpected scenarios were on top of my son being the younger brother to a sister with Down syndrome. Clearly, her unique needs required more attention than some other situations. Did our attention going to her impact him?

Even if those circumstances had been different, he was still being raised by a father whose primary attachment pathway is one of anxious attachment. It was well past his 10th birthday before I became aware of my patterns.

How we love today is a direct reflection of how we were loved yesterday. How we will love tomorrow will be the byproduct of how we choose to love today.

Time will tell what primary patterns my son develops as he grows into adulthood, but it would be completely understandable if he has some non-secure pathways, even though he has two parents who love him as much as any parent can love.

As he grows, my son will have to do the work to discover his own tendencies. Chances are that some ways he has learned to cope as a child won't be fruitful ways to approach relationships as an adult. What saves us in previous relationships can kill us in present ones. Attachment Theory helps us understand why something worked in the past but doesn't work now. And it empowers us to make different choices.

This is where the true power lies, not in blaming others for our actions, but understanding the climate in which our relational strategies were formed and finding what needs to be reformed for healthier relationships.

Far from offering excuses, Attachment Theory provides a sense of empowerment. Without understanding who we are and how we became us, we will forever live enslaved to our earliest patterns. Yet when we understand our story, it allows us to change.

You and I had no choice in how our earliest needs were met. We were utterly dependent on others, and our brains responded to their actions, forming our relational pathways. However, we are not limited to those pathways. We have the agency to create new routes, understand new strategies, and develop different patterns.

Imagine navigating a cross-country trip using a 1995 Rand McNally Map. That would be crazy. A lot has changed in three decades, and the fastest route in the mid-90s from one city to another likely isn't the fastest route today. Using the Rand McNally made sense back then, but it would be foolish to use it today.

Yet that's exactly what many of us do when it comes to relationships. The routes we formed in childhood to be seen and connected are the same strategies we use today. Thankfully, there is a better way.

You didn't choose your early wiring. But you get to choose what happens next.

**Attachment Theory
isn't about pointing fingers,
it's about pointing forward.**

The past shaped us, but with understanding and empathy, it doesn't have to define us.

THE MEMORIES WE DON'T REMEMBER

If one objection to attachment is the fear that we will blame our parents and use it as an excuse, another objection stems from a lack of understanding of how much our past influences our present.

It feels like my childhood experiences have no lasting impact on my daily life. It's also hard to believe that things I can't remember—my first few years of life—could have such tremendous influence over who I am.

Many object by saying the past doesn't matter. They object to the idea that past emotional needs could have negative impacts in the present. But here's the truth: the past does matter, even when we can't remember it. The past might matter even more when we can't remember it because it allows previous situations to impact the present without us being aware of their influence.

Dan Siegel teaches that memories fall into two broad categories: explicit and implicit.[3] Both influence how we form relationships and respond to others, but they do so in very different ways.

Explicit memories are the ones we typically think of when we hear the word *memory*. They're stored in our brains as past events we can recall on demand. If I ask you what you ate for lunch last Tuesday, you might pause, think, and say, "Taco salad." You know you're remembering something that happened before. That's an explicit memory.

Implicit memories, on the other hand, are stored without our conscious awareness. They come from experiences that happened before our brains could form explicit memories. So instead of remembering them as "that happened back then," we *feel* them in our bodies and emotions, often without understanding why.

Neurologically, the brain isn't developed enough to form explicit memories until around age four. That's why most of us don't have clear, story-like memories from before preschool. But that doesn't mean those early years didn't leave a mark. They did, just in a different way.

In fact, our brains begin storing implicit memories as early as the seventh month of pregnancy. That means even before birth, our nervous systems are taking in experiences, especially emotional ones like stress, safety, or danger. These get stored deep in our body's memory system.

So what's the key difference?

Explicit memories feel like *the past*.

Implicit memories feel like *the present*.

With explicit memory, you *know* you're remembering. With implicit memory, you're reacting to a past experience, but it feels like it's happening *right now*. This is a crucial distinction in understanding emotional responses and patterns we may not be able to explain.

This difference is especially important in relationships. You may find yourself reacting strongly to something minor: a facial expression, a tone of voice, a smell, or even a pause in conversation. What feels like an overreaction may actually be an accurate reaction to something your nervous system stored long ago. In these moments, your body is doing what it was designed to do: protect you. The only problem is, it doesn't always know the threat has passed.

Siegel shares a story that illustrates how implicit memory works. He was working with a young boy who had been severely abused by his father. The abuse stopped. The father went to prison. For years, the boy seemed to thrive.

Then, one school year, something changed. The boy became dysregulated—anxious, aggressive, and fearful every morning as he entered the classroom. His teachers and caregivers were baffled. Was it puberty? Social stress? Something else?

Siegel dug deeper. Eventually, he discovered something subtle but significant: the boy's new male teacher wore Old Spice aftershave, the same scent his father had used during the abuse. Without realizing it, the boy's nervous system remembered. The smell triggered his implicit memory of danger, even though he had no conscious recollection of the connection.[4]

WHAT I IMAGINE MY STORY TO BE

My childhood was one of being well-loved but not always well-seen. My parents cared deeply for me, but their marriage carried stress that often turned them inward. They divorced when I was four, remarried each other when I was in first grade, and finally divorced again when I was in college.

But imagine me at one year old. My dad had moved out for

a season, and my mom was left to carry the weight of two small kids and her own heartache. I had just taken my first steps, said my first words, and was learning to explore my world. Yet suddenly, my dad wasn't around as much. My little brain didn't understand why. All I knew was to stay on alert, listening for the door, wondering if he would show up today.

Meanwhile, my mom was doing her best, but she was exhausted. At times, my needs went unseen, not because she didn't love me, but because she simply didn't have the emotional capacity for everything life demanded in that season. And at other times, when she did scoop me up, it may not have been to soothe me but to soothe herself. I was wrapped in her love, yes, but also in her stress. Even without words, my body absorbed both.

This is how attachment forms. A child doesn't think

through these things; they feel them. My body learned
to be on guard: look for him, watch out for her, stay alert
to what could happen. Love was beautiful, but it wasn't
always predictable. Sometimes it was there. Sometimes it
wasn't.

THE BODY REMEMBERS WHAT THE MIND CAN'T

Even though we can't remember our earliest experiences,
we can understand how they shape us. As trauma expert
Bessel van der Kolk puts it, *"The body keeps the score."*[5]
In the previous story with the boy who was abused, as he
entered a new grade, he wasn't thinking about the past, but
his body was reliving it. The teacher changed aftershave
lotions, the boy's body relaxed, and the school year went on
without incident.

Even though we can't recall our early childhood in story form, those years shape how we see the world, ourselves, and others. The emotional environment—whether safe and nurturing or inconsistent and frightening—is stored in our bodies as implicit memory. And those early, unspoken experiences often become the lens through which we interpret new situations.

This is one reason why self-awareness and emotional regulation are vital. When we pause long enough to get curious about our strong reactions, we create space to respond instead of just reacting. We begin to ask better questions: *What is my body remembering? What might this feeling really be about?*

When we ask those kinds of questions without judgment, we begin to write a new story, one in which the past no longer controls the present and healing becomes possible.

CHAPTER 2:

SECURE ATTACHMENT

Ava's Story

Ava knew she had a good childhood, but she assumed it was the normal experience of most children. Her parents loved her. Her brother irritated her. Her grandparents doted on her.

Her parents weren't exceptional. They both worked hard, but sometimes money was a struggle. They would disagree on how to raise the kids and occasionally forget who was picking Ava up at soccer or who was getting her brother from karate. However, when they lost their temper or failed to meet an obligation, they would always come back to apologize. Hugs were exchanged. Life continued.

Ava remembers a specific time in third grade when she and her mother got into a fight. Ava was supposed to brush her teeth, but didn't. Then, she lied about it. When her mom found the dry toothbrush, she lost her temper. When it was all over, Ava ran to her room in tears. Ten minutes passed and her mom gently knocked on her bedroom door. She came in and sat on the floor. "I overreacted. I'm sorry," her mom said. She then explained that she wants to help Ava take care of herself, but that sometimes as a mom she loses sight of the big picture. She asked Ava if they could try again tomorrow. Once again hugs were given and as her mom left the room, Ava felt a sense of calm.

Her dad was a man of few words, but always full of love. On hard days, he would bring her favorite candy. He would regularly tell her, "You don't have to be the best, you just need to try your best." Every night, he would come by her room, hug her, and remind her of his love for her.

Now in her thirties, Ava is a teacher, mom of two, and married to a great man. She has a better understanding of her parents and a deeper appreciation of what they gave to her and her brother. Ava isn't a perfect parent. Their marriage hasn't always been ideal. They've faced job transitions, fertility struggles, and the chaos of the toddler years. But a decade into marriage, they have a solid footing. There is confidence about the years to come and an excitement of how much more they will learn and grow.

Ava openly talks about her emotions with her husband and friends. She laughs easily, forgives quickly, and sets clear boundaries when needed. She doesn't feel anxious when someone is going through their own issue or when a person disagrees with her. She assumes the best in people until proven otherwise. She knows she is loved and that others can generally be trusted. She doesn't strive to earn love. She lives from it.

That's what secure attachment is about.

WHAT IS SECURE ATTACHMENT?

Secure attachment is a relational state where a person consistently experiences emotional safety within the context of intimate relationships. Julie Menanno emphasizes that a secure attachment is not just understood, it's "felt."[6]

Dan Siegel writes that being secure is the byproduct of feeling "seen, soothed, and safe." When combined, they become the 4 S's—seen, soothed, safe, and secure—which Siegel references regarding attachment.[7] These are needs present at birth that continue through the life span.

Secure attachment is not the byproduct of perfection. Often, it is the result of presence—physical, emotional, and relational presence. Consider Ainsworth's Infant Strange Scenario, which we discussed earlier. When children were securely attached, they experienced both independence and connection. They were free to explore while also having the reassurance of their caregiver. They could leverage their mom or dad's presence to interpret new places or strange people. They could depend upon their caregiver to calm them when they were dysregulated. They felt safe because of their presence.

In a secure attachment, a child learns to recognize themselves and others. They experience agency and bonding. They value themselves and others. They can distinguish themselves as separate from others while also belonging to something bigger than themselves.

In adulthood, secure attachment looks like this:

- I believe I am lovable.
- I believe others are generally trustworthy.
- I can express my needs without fear.
- I can manage emotions without collapsing or exploding.
- I can handle both intimacy and autonomy.

Secure attachment does not require perfection, but it is the result of a consistency from those who mean the most to us. Their consistent responses help regulate our emotions.

WHAT SECURE ATTACHMENT LOOKS LIKE IN REAL LIFE

Secure attachment isn't just an internal feeling; it's a way of showing up. It shapes how people love, lead, work, parent, and relate. The securely attached adult lives from a grounded sense of self, the capacity to trust others, and a belief that relationships—even imperfect ones—can be safe and enduring.

The following pages show how secure attachment expresses itself across key adult life domains. Read each chart slowly and compare with your actions when you are at your best and when you are at your worst.

1. Romantic Relationships

BEHAVIOR	EXPRESSION	UNDERLYING STRENGTH
Emotional Presence	Fully engaged with intimacy and affection	Confidence in connection
Direct Communication	Expresses needs clearly and listens well	Belief that communication is safe
Conflict Engagement	Doesn't avoid or escalate	Trusts that repair is possible
Balanced Independence	Closeness without control or fear of loss	Self-assurance

Insight: Securely attached partners are not perfect, but they show up. They don't need to be chased or coaxed for connection; they are emotionally accessible and accountable.

2. Friendships

BEHAVIOR	EXPRESSION	UNDERLYING STRENGTH
Mutuality	Gives and receives support without imbalance	Healthy boundaries and reciprocity
Low Reactivity	Responds calmly to silence or space	Internal stability
Emotional Honesty	Shares openly without oversharing	Trust in being accepted

Insight: Securely attached adults enjoy friendships as life-giving rather than identity-defining. They aren't ruled by social anxiety or people-pleasing.

3. Parenting

BEHAVIOR	EXPRESSION	UNDERLYING STRENGTH
Emotional Attunement	Reads child's cues and responds appropriately	Trust in the parent-child bond
Consistency and Repair	Shows up, owns mistakes, makes things right	Believes love isn't lost in failure
Emotional Modeling	Demonstrates regulation and honesty	Capacity for self-regulation

Insight: Secure parents teach their children that emotions are welcome and relationships can withstand mistakes. They parent with steadiness, not control.

4. Work and Achievement

BEHAVIOR	EXPRESSION	UNDERLYING STRENGTH
Comfortable with feedback	Doesn't personalize critique	Internal security
Balanced Identity	Values work but isn't defined by it	Clear sense of self
Collaborative	Works well with others, gives and receives input	Capacity for self-regulation

Insight: Secure adults work from a place of purpose, not pressure. They can lead or follow with humility and presence.

5. Faith and Spirituality

BEHAVIOR	EXPRESSION	UNDERLYING STRENGTH
Honest spiritual life	Shares doubts and praises freely	Feels safe in relationship with God
Relational prayer	Engages with God as present and attentive	Trust in God's goodness
Collaborative	Doesn't lose faith during hardship	Secure base beyond the self

Insight: Securely attached individuals don't hide from God. They wrestle honestly, pray openly, and receive grace without resistance.

16 CHARACTERISTICS OF SECURE ATTACHMENT

One of the things that strikes me as I travel the country speaking on relationships is how often someone will come up to me after a talk and say, "I thought I had a good marriage, but now I don't know." It's never my intention to create doubt in people's minds; however, in many of these conversations, I learn that what people think is normal isn't always normal. Many people grow up without a model of a healthy relationship and sometimes what they have experienced becomes their definition of normal, or even healthy. In many cases, that experience is far from it.

Here is a selection of some characteristics of secure attachment in marriage. It's not an exhaustive list. It's not intended to be a perfect list. It's simply a quick list of some ideas that I use to help people understand what a healthy relationship looks like.

---

1. Trust: I know you will treat my heart right.

Trust is the foundation of friendship. It's a belief that another person's intention is for my good, and their general relationship skill level can lead to a positive outcome for me. It's not an expectation of perfection, but it is a confident belief in good intent. And a significant part of trust is knowing that if they get it wrong, they will feel remorse and will make it right.

Trust demands time to grow. It can be quickly lost, but never quickly gained. Consistently telling the truth, proving oneself trustworthy, and building a life of integrity and love allows both partners to trust one another.

2. Respect: I value your opinion.

If trust is about another's heart, respect is about their mind and capabilities. To respect another is to believe they will act in an honorable and noble way. It's to know they have skills and abilities that can add to your life. Respect is most easily seen in whether another person can influence you. If we take their words to heart, showing caution when they encourage caution, and boldness when they push us forward, then respect is present.

Respectful relationships are reciprocal relationships. They can depend on each other, leading where I am strong and my partner is weak, and following when my partner is strong and I am weak.

3. Vulnerability: Will you hold me?

When trust and respect are present, a person can be vulnerable. Secure attachment empowers a person to know when they can be vulnerable and when they can't. It enables them to open up to others, connect with them, and protect themselves from exposing their vulnerabilities to people who might harm them.

Whereas avoidant pathways restrict all vulnerability, and anxious pathways lead us to be vulnerable with people who shouldn't be trusted, secure attachment empowers healthy vulnerability. Consider one spouse saying to another, "Will you hold me?" This is a sign of vulnerability. It's saying, "I'm in need and I'm asking you to help me."

4. Exploration: Let's go see.

Remember in the Infant Strange Scenario how some children would eventually warm to the new environment and explore the toys in the room? That's secure attachment. It empowers us to explore beyond ourselves and our relationship. When attachment needs are unmet, we must fixate on getting them met. Yet when we feel seen, loved, and secure, we can look toward other things.

We can try new hobbies, consider new friendships, learn new skills, and enjoy novel experiences. Without fear of failure or isolation, curiosity can guide us into uncharted territory. This exploration can be inside the individual, between the couple, or together, beyond the relationship.

5. Emotional Regulation:
I can feel without being ruled by every feeling.

Secure attachment rescues a person from two misappropriations of emotion. An anxious pathway can be ruled by emotion, unable to use logic to discern any given feeling. In contrast, an avoidant pathway might be void of emotion, unable to recognize the emotions underneath their logic and actions. Secure attachment allows us to feel, while also preventing us from being enslaved by every feeling. We recognize the role we play in regulating emotion so that it is leveraged in the right way and doesn't wreak havoc on our lives.

It empowers individuals to self-regulate and couples to co-regulate.

6. Communication:
Here's what I want to say. What do you want to say?

Assertive communication is the byproduct of secure attachment. We avoid passive, aggressive, or passive-aggressive language, and instead clearly state what we think, believe, feel, and desire without creating a climate where others can't freely state their opinions. We neither hold back aspects of our hearts nor overwhelm others with our forcefulness.

It makes communication easier, in part, because it gives space for poor communication. We all communicate poorly at times. Where secure attachment is absent, failures in communication carry a greater weight. Where it is present, a couple can navigate the failure because they hear the heart more than the words.

7. Empathy: I see you.

Whereas non-secure attachment causes us to overly fixate on self, secure attachment frees us to see one another. We have compassion and grace toward others without excusing bad behavior or overlooking harm. Empathy doesn't require complete understanding. It simply offers presence, curiosity, and compassion during both calm and conflict.

Empathy is easier when attachments are strong because we know it will be reciprocated in our time of need. While an avoidant pathway might struggle to see (or admit) their need and an anxious pathway might appear to be empathetic while actually serving the other person as a way to earn their affection, secure attachment frees us to truly leverage our resources for another person.

8. Flexibility: We can bend without breaking.

Siegel says rigidity is one of the opposites of secure attachment (chaos is the other).[7] Having a strong bond allows couples to be flexible. While they have their preferred outcomes and standard operating procedures, they can adapt to unique circumstances without hindering their connection.

Because the relationship is the foundational piece of their lives, they can quickly adapt to circumstances that change—a job loss, diagnosis, change in season, unexpected life event, etc. Without a strong connection, couples are hesitant to risk any external change, lacking the confidence that the relationship can endure. A strong connection invites couples toward change because their connection goes beyond their present circumstances.

9. Stability: I know who I am (and who we are).

The balance of flexibility is stability. Non-secure attachment creates a distance within oneself, which also prevents a connection between the couple. When you don't truly know or appreciate who you are, it's difficult to allow someone else to love you.

Secure attachment gives a sense of identity beyond job titles, family roles, or personal achievements. Knowing who you are creates stability in one's life and relationships. This binds the couple together, creating a firm foundation from which everything else in life is built. While circumstances can change, the couple's bond remains. Stability is an emotional, mental, and spiritual reality.

10. Resilience: We will make it through this.

Secure couples don't always avoid pain, but they continually repair through it. They keep their connection close, which gives them resilience across the life stages. They face adversity with unity. They lean into one another during tough times rather than isolating. Conflict and stress are leveraged to strengthen their relationship rather than tear them apart.

The Serenity Prayer reminds us that "hardship is the pathway to peace." Secure couples experience the truth of this prayer. They face hard times with hope. They know the difficult times can, in the end, become the most beautiful times because of how it develops their character and love.

11. Healthy Thirds: We are better because of others and others are better because of us.

Healthy couples don't isolate. They integrate. Friends, families, coworkers, faith communities, neighbors, and acquaintances are welcome and enriching. They use their love for each other in a way that benefits those around them. And they allow others around them to strengthen their connection with each other.

Non-secure attachment creates a rightful skepticism of others. Where a secure attachment is absent, others become a threat. If our attachment needs aren't met within the marriage, we might seek to have them met outside the marriage.

When others benefit our connection and our connection benefits others, we are characterized by a secure attachment.

12. Support: She/he is my biggest cheerleader.

When I love Jenny well, I see more in her than she sees in herself. I am more for her than I am even for myself. Secure attachment frees us to the truth that when our spouse flourishes, it's better for the whole family.

Non-secure attachment can see the success of our spouse as a threat to us. If we feel unseen, their success makes us feel more invisible. However, secure attachment doesn't feel threatened by others, especially not by our spouse. This allows us to cheer each other on. In a secure attachment, both spouses care more about the success of the other than themselves.

13. Shared Goals: We are creating the life we want.

When we are bonded with one another in healthy ways, we feel empowered to direct our future. It creates the desire and habit of hoping, dreaming, and communicating what could be. But these don't remain simply as desires; they are turned into practical steps of how to make our dreams come true. They become shared goals.

Non-secure attachment prevents couples from having the safety and vulnerability to ask "what could we become?" It forces them to focus on the present, preventing them from considering the future. But secure attachment lifts our eyes toward the horizon, helps us define what we want, and then partners us with each other to make it happen.

14. Conflict Resolution: Help me understand.

Secure couples don't fear disagreement. They engage it respectfully. They focus on solving the problem, not attacking the person. They think in "gray" when needed, and they return to repair when emotions run high. Rather than trying to make their point, they seek first to understand the point of the other. Understanding is their focus, not *"winning."*

Non-secure couples are unable to resolve conflict. Topics are avoided, conversations aren't had, and discussions that do happen do not result in progress. Where attachment is strong, conflict leads to even stronger connection; where it is weak, conflict further weakens the bond.

15. Physical Intimacy: I love being intimate with you.

Healthy couples value intimacy both inside and outside the bedroom. They leverage their physical bodies for the well-being of one another. Their physical connection is both a byproduct of their emotional connection and a source of that connection. They prioritize and value one another.

Non-secure attachment divides the bedroom. Neither spouse can fully please the other, as they are fixated on their own safety and meeting their own needs. Likewise, when expressed, non-secure pathways can lead to inappropriate sexual contact because we are seeking a connection via sex rather than expressing a connection that is already present.

16. Positive Outlook: We are better together.

At the core of a secure marriage is hope. These couples speak life over one another. They enjoy each other. They believe their best years are ahead, even when circumstances are difficult. Joy is not reserved for the easy days. It's part of the everyday foundation. They are grateful and allow their gratitude to flow into generosity for one another and others.

Non-secure couples struggle for such an outlook. They question, doubt, and become skeptical about each other and themselves. They consider or even fantasize about life apart or with another. Their disconnection is a constant drain on their hope for tomorrow.

Ultimately, when I think of secure attachment, the best definition may be Galatians 5:22-23: *"The fruit of the*

Spirit is love, joy, peace, patience, kindness, goodness, faithfulness, gentleness, and self-control. " These different aspects combine to define one whole, that one whole defines secure attachment.

CONTRASTS WITH NON-SECURE ATTACHMENT

Secure attachment doesn't mean the absence of insecurity. It means having the tools to navigate it wisely. While anxious, avoidant, and disorganized pathways often form as strategies to manage fear, secure attachment grows from repeated experiences of safety, trust, and repair.

Here's how secure attachment contrasts with the other styles:

ATTACHMENT STYLE	CORE BELIEF	RESPONSE TO THREAT	RELATIONAL IMPACT
Secure	"We can work through this."	Stay, name, repair	Offers and receives love with steadiness
Anxious	"You will leave me."	Cling, over-function	Seeks constant reassurance, feels fragile
Avoidant	"You will control me."	Withdraw, minimize	Detaches from needs and intimacy
Disorganized	"You will hurt me."	Flip between cling and withdraw	Chaotic, confusing relational patterns

Secure attachment doesn't eliminate fear. It simply knows how to face it. Instead of reacting, a secure pathway invites us to respond with presence and perspective. It doesn't require us to deny pain, but it prevents us from panicking because of the pain.

Securely attached individuals are not reactive to stress in relationships; they are responsive. They don't need to control others, fix everything, or protect themselves through detachment. They assume relationships can survive imperfection because they've lived it.

And, perhaps most importantly, they offer a stabilizing presence to those with insecure patterns. They don't absorb chaos, but they don't abandon it either. They stay present, grounded, and kind, even when others are struggling.

THE NERVOUS SYSTEM & SECURE ATTACHMENT

Secure attachment doesn't just shape how we feel. It determines how the body responds. It forms when a child experiences consistent co-regulation from caregivers, which trains the brain and body to return to safety even in stress. This lays the groundwork for what Siegel calls "integration": the healthy coordination of body, brain, and relationships.[9]

God designed our nervous systems to seek connection and return to a state of peace. When we experience safe relationships, we reflect the relational wholeness God intended from the beginning.

Securely attached individuals live primarily in what's often called the safe and social mode (as opposed to fight, flight, freeze, or fawn). In this state, the body feels calm, connected, and curious. Heart rate is steady, breath is deep, muscles are relaxed, and the mind is alert but not hypervigilant.

When faced with distress, securely attached people may briefly enter sympathetic arousal (fight or flight) or shutdown (freeze), but they return to regulation more quickly. Why? Because they've internalized a template of co-regulation, they don't fear their own emotional activation.

THE SHAME CYCLE THAT NEVER TAKES HOLD

In nonsecure attachment styles, shame often becomes the dominant internal driver:

- "I'm too much."
- "I'm not enough."
- "I will be left, controlled, or exposed."

But in secure attachment, shame has a ceiling. It exists (it's part of being human) but it does not define the self.

Secure individuals still feel guilt when they do wrong, embarrassment when they fall short, or insecurity when they fail. But they don't collapse into identity-based shame. They don't believe their value depends on flawlessness. They can say:

- "I made a mistake, but I am not a mistake."
- "I feel awkward, but I'm still worthy of love."
- "I failed, but I am not a failure."

This is not arrogance; it's grace. It's the fruit of growing up in relationships where failure was met with care, emotions were met with regulation, and return was always possible. And if that wasn't present in early life, secure attachment can still form through consistent adult experiences of attuned presence and safe love.

Where nonsecure attachment says, "I must earn love," secure attachment says, "Love will meet me here even when I'm a mess."

This is what the gospel announces: that we are deeply flawed yet deeply loved (Romans 5:8). Secure attachment reflects the same paradox: not perfection, but presence; not shame, but grace.

AVA REVISITED

Ava's life still includes stress, disappointment, and emotional complexity. Sometimes she excessively worries about relationships and on other occasions she emotionally avoids stressful situations. She's not perfect. But she does have a primary secure attachment so she can more easily let go of the worry or lean back into the situation she's been avoiding.

In her mid-30s, she's parenting two children, balancing work as a teacher, and walking with her husband through his aging mother's decline. Life isn't easy. But her relationships are steady. They have conflicts and frustrations, but Ava has a steadiness many others lack. She has a strong sense of self, a good trust in others, and an expectation that life will generally go her way, even though some circumstances will be difficult.

When she and her husband argue, they make up. When the kids melt down, she can separate her inner life from their outward frustrations. When she feels overwhelmed, she can ask for help.

Her friendships are life-giving, but they aren't identity-shaping. Who she is comes from something greater than what she does or what others think of her. Her prayer life is honest, not an attempt to earn God's favor. In every situation and scenario, Ava is the same person—honest, humble, hard-working, and present.

She experiences fear, but she's not ruled by it. She has flaws, but she's not defined by them. She experiences the sorrows of life, but she's not undone by them. Ava lives from a place of trust, presence, and good dependence. She's a good example of where secure attachment comes from and what it is. Not perfection, but a generally good ability to connect in spite of the hardships and failures in life.

Ava's story isn't just about human resilience. It's about grace. She's been formed by people, yes, but also by a God who holds her steady. Her life reflects a rootedness that can only come from knowing she is loved by something greater than her failure or success.

CHAPTER 3:

THE THREE PATHWAYS OF NON-SECURE ATTACHMENT

ANXIOUS ATTACHMENT: WHEN LOVE FEELS FRAGILE

Second Grade Memories

When I was in second grade, mornings were hard. Most nights I slept fine, but as soon as I woke up for school, I was nervous. I'd try to hold back tears. If my mom asked what was wrong, my best explanation was, "I might get in trouble today." I never actually did. But every morning felt like the day it might happen.

If everything went smoothly, I could mostly hold it together. But if anything was off, it was too much. I remember one morning there was nothing for me to take for lunch. My dad said, "Just eat at school." But for me, that wasn't an option. I was a picky eater, and that might as well have meant, "Skip lunch." My mom understood, but she had to get to work. So my dad went to a convenience store, brought back a few items, none of which I liked. I didn't expect him to know what I wanted, but I couldn't figure out why he was frustrated that I still wasn't satisfied.

Now as a parent, I look back with great empathy for my parents. Life was busy. They were juggling a lot. They loved me and wanted me to be okay, but they didn't always have the time or tools to stop and prioritize my emotions. They were trying to get through the day. But as a kid, I drew a quiet conclusion: *My emotions are a burden. Contain them so no one else has to deal with them. And if someone does give me attention, I should feel guilty for needing it.*

It's no wonder I grew into adulthood struggling to identify my feelings. The emotions are there but often buried. When they finally come out, I still feel guilty for needing help. This is the anxious pathway. It's the inner script that says:

- "I'm too much."
- "My needs are inconvenient."
- "If I'm seen, I'll only be a burden."

Anxious attachment often doesn't start with abuse or neglect. It can form in well-loved homes where parents are busy, stressed, or stretched thin. Kids learn to manage their own needs, but the cost is a body always on alert and a heart unsure if love will stay steady.

Here's how childhood experiences like that play out years later.

CARLOS'S STORY

Growing up, Carlos considered his family solid. They were affectionate, hardworking, and emotionally present. His mom called him her "sweet boy," and his dad was a quiet provider who showed love through consistency and hard work. At times, things were tense, but Carlos knew that was true in every family. When his mom was upset, he had a unique ability to calm her down. When his dad was distant, Carlos could draw him back in. He was a great kid who was consistently praised for his success—good grades, a clean room, and very few needs. In Carlos's mind, when you love someone, you stay alert, adjust as necessary, and do your part to keep the peace.

He learned early that relationships required effort, especially emotional effort. If someone didn't respond right away, it meant something. If a friend pulled back, he had likely done something to create the distance. If his mom wasn't happy, it was his job to calm her. If his dad was disengaged, it was Carlos's job to reengage him. If love didn't seem steady, he assumed he needed to work harder to earn it.

So when he met Sofia, he brought the same energy into his romantic relationship that he had experienced in his family of origin. At first, she loved it. He was so attentive, quick to reply, and his desire to be close felt amazing. But as months passed, she felt exhausted. Carlos always needed to be reassured that things were good. He would sometimes doubt or question her if her schedule was just a little off.

If she wanted some time alone, he would take it personally. If she was having a bad day, he would think he had done something to cause it. To Sofia, things that were nothing were often seen as something very significant to Carlos. She sometimes wondered, "Why doesn't he trust me?" But she didn't dare bring it up out of fear of it devastating Carlos.

Sofia loved Carlos, but she could sense things with him were different than how she grew up. Her home was calm and secure. Her parents were predictable, but never rigid. The best was always assumed, and Sofia never doubted her parents' love. But it often felt like Carlos doubted her love. He would continually second-guess her feelings. And Carlos struggled to understand why Sofia couldn't see the obvious warning signs he saw.

It wasn't until premarital counseling that Carlos began to realize that some of the things which seemed so natural to him may not be as healthy as he thought.

Anxious Attachment sounded like someone was reading his mind. Sofia didn't worry constantly, she didn't chase connections, and she expected safety. What felt odd to Carlos, he now heard, was actually normal and healthy. Carlos's assumption that love was fragile, his continual fear of losing Sofia's love, and his worry of *being too much* weren't signs that he truly cared. What he thought was love, was actually fear in disguise.

Carlos had a primary pathway of anxious attachment.

WHAT IS ANXIOUS ATTACHMENT?

Anxious attachment is one of the three primary non-secure attachment styles (alongside avoidant and disorganized), developed in early childhood to navigate inconsistent caregiving. Children with anxious attachment often experience unpredictable caregiving, sometimes responsive, sometimes neglectful. The child becomes hypervigilant to any changes in emotional availability, developing a belief that love is unreliable and must be pursued or earned.

Rather than feeling safe to explore the world, anxiously attached individuals stay emotionally tethered to caregivers (and later, partners), driven by a need for reassurance.

Core Beliefs of Anxious Attachment:

- "I am not enough to keep someone's love."
- "Others will leave me."
- "I must try harder to be lovable."
- "Closeness can be lost at any moment."

You don't think these beliefs; you feel them. They are not just ideas in your head; they are stored in your body. They were shaped by early experiences and reinforced in adulthood.

How Anxious Attachment Shows Up
(and How to Grow Through It)

DOMAIN	EXPRESSION	TRIGGER	DEFAULT REACTION	HEALING MOVE
Romantic Love	Clinging, fear of loss	Emotional distance	Protest behaviors (over-texting, seeking reassurance)	Secure communication, body regulation
Friendship	Over-giving, jealousy	Perceived neglect	Anxiety, withdrawal, resentment	Assert needs, seek reciprocity
Parenting	Enmeshment, over-identification	Child's independence	Emotional over-involvement	Balance presence with boundaries
Work	People-pleasing, burnout	Criticism, unmet expectations	Self-doubt, overworking	Internal validation, boundary-setting
Faith/ Spirituality	Works-based identity	Feeling unworthy of grace	Spiritual performance	Receive unconditional love, rest in grace

The Nervous System & Anxious Attachment

Siegel's work reminds us, "The way we use our minds can change our brains."[10] That includes our attachment wiring. Anxious attachment reflects a nervous system that is overactivated, tilted toward sympathetic arousal (fight or flight) even in non-threatening situations. Something as simple as a delayed text can be terrifying because the brain interprets delay as distance. And distance feels dangerous.

This physiological state makes anxious individuals excellent at detecting subtle shifts but terrible at resting in emotional security.[11] It can express itself in anxiety, racing thoughts, urgency, scanning for rejection or abandonment, mood swings, rumination, and a need for others to calm us. Simply, it leads to dysregulation. Their emotional thermostat isn't regulating the temperature. They always believe a relationship needs to be warmed, because they fear the cold.

The Shame Spiral

Growth occurs not through shame but through curiosity and compassion. Anxiously attached individuals often battle a powerful inner critic that says:

- **"Why can't I just be normal?"**
- **"I ruin every relationship."**
- **"I'm too much."**

This shame perpetuates the anxious cycle. But when curiosity meets compassion, integration begins. The anxious part of us isn't a villain; it's a child who once had to work too hard for love. And as we begin to see that child the way God always saw that child—as loved, welcomed, and wanted—the anxious pathway can be traded for a secure one. In *The Soul of Shame*, Dr. Curt Thompson shows that "We can only be known to the degree that we are seen and loved in the midst of our shame."[12]

Path Toward Secure Attachment

Healing anxious attachment isn't about becoming perfectly "secure." It's about becoming more aware, more compassionate, and more regulated.

Awareness helps us notice what's happening inside before we react outside.

Compassion helps us hold our story with kindness rather than shame.

Regulation gives us the ability to calm our body when our heart feels unsafe.

Growth happens in small moments. It's not dramatic steps forward, but small gains when we pause our panic and remind ourselves of the truth, when we breathe and choose a different way.

Practices that Foster Growth:

PRACTICE	WHY IT HELPS
Self-soothing	Builds internal safety without needing others immediately
Body awareness	Recognizes anxiety signals before they spiral
Mindful relationships	Identifies secure patterns, learns from them
Counseling	Repairs attachment injuries in a safe environment
Naming needs openly	Breaks the cycle of hinting or testing
Boundary work	Builds self-trust without over-relying on others
Secure partner/ friendships	Stability rewires our relational expectations

Key Insight: You don't have to stop caring.
You just need to know you are safe when you do care.

A Reframed Narrative

Instead of telling themselves, "I'm too needy," those with anxious attachment can learn to say:

- **"My longing makes sense."**
- **"My body is remembering something old."**
- **"I can care deeply without clinging."**
- **"I can name what I need without apologizing."**

David Daniels, professor of psychiatry at Stanford University, reminds us, "Emotional states of our early years become the states within us that come to be our internal experience of ourselves later on."[13] But with awareness, we're not locked into that old way of thinking.

CARLOS REVISITED

Carlos is still learning, but he has made significant progress since first understanding attachment theory in his premarital class. He's discovering that what felt "normal" to him growing up wasn't the way love had to be. He didn't have to earn love or over-function for it. It wasn't necessary to always scan for disconnection or continually monitor the emotions of others to see how he might have messed up. He didn't have to internalize responsibility for everyone else. It allowed him to navigate his family of origin. Yes, he loved his parents, but his love was complicated by his fear.

With Sofia's help and the safety of their relationship, he started to let his guard down. He's sharing more of his heart even as he learns to soothe himself. Whenever he notices himself fixating on what Sofia needs to do to improve the relationship, he catches himself. He redirects his attention to his own actions and his power to change. When she needs space, he no longer panics. When tensions rise, he's confident that they will be able to navigate the conflict. When she says, "We're okay," he's beginning to believe her.

He's not a radically different man. He's still sensitive to Sofia and others. He's still very gifted at reading a room and seeing a need long before others recognize it. However, he's improving and acknowledging that the needs and frustrations of others often have nothing to do with him.

For the first time, Carlos is finding a kind of love that doesn't demand anxiety to maintain. He's learning to love for love's sake rather than loving as a way to navigate his fear. He's on his way toward a more secure pathway.

AVOIDANT ATTACHMENT: THE FEAR OF BEING TRAPPED

CLAIRE'S STORY

If you ask Claire, she had an uneventful childhood. Her family was good. She was loved. Her life was no different than anyone else's. Claire saw her parents as responsible, orderly, and stable. Her mom was on top of everything. The house was perfect. She rarely raised her voice. She was a mom-machine. Her dad was loving, ever-present. He showed up to every game, worked hard, and taught Claire the important things to succeed in life. They loved her, and she was sure of it.

Claire was grateful her parents taught her to be self-sufficient, confident, and not overwhelmed by emotions. But if Claire could look back, she would notice something. When she cried, the room went quiet. Her mom would try to fix things quickly, and her dad would quietly leave the room. Comfort was something she never experienced. But, as a child and now an adult, she never knew that comfort was something she deserved or needed. "Take a breath" and "Be strong" seemed like good parenting techniques. Learning to handle her problems and not dwell on them seemed like a gift.

So, Claire learned to manage life on her own. She excelled in school, sports, and nearly everything she tried. While she appeared so confident and self-assured, her friends often seemed like an emotional mess. Her parents praised her for her independence, maturity, and self-discipline. And she saw her friends who "needed" a boyfriend as a kind of failure.

She dated. Had fun. But oftentimes, the boys in her life became too needy, the relationships became too demanding, and she would move on. Any commitment to a man seemed like a roadblock to the life she wanted. When someone got too close, she would find a reason to break off the relationship and move on.

And she could move on quickly. While her friends were heartbroken when relationships ended, Claire felt liberated. While new relationships were fun, the longer they went, the unhappier she got. Few things excited Claire like the freedom of a good breakup.

Then she met Daniel.

He was kind, consistent, and calm. He asked questions and actually waited for the answers. He didn't mind her need for space. He wouldn't chase her when she pulled away. He would often say, "I'm here when you are ready."

At first, Claire found his steadiness confusing. But over time, it felt uncomfortable. In every relationship before Daniel, Claire had clearly been in control. She set the relationship climate, and when past boyfriends didn't like it, she would be done with them. But she didn't have that power over Daniel, and it confused her. He clearly liked her, but she didn't rule his life.

She felt herself falling in love with him, but that didn't just make her feel uncomfortable; it terrified her. She would pull him close, but then push him away. Yet he was consistent. And she could feel there was something so right about his presence and something a little off about her fickleness.

Daniel didn't demand her vulnerability, but his authenticity began to reveal a guardedness she didn't want to have. For the first time, she began to wonder: "Maybe it's okay to need someone. Maybe logic alone isn't enough for a good life."

What Is Avoidant Attachment?

Avoidant attachment starts when love feels distant. It doesn't mean our caregivers were cruel, but they weren't emotionally close either. When children experience rejection, distance, or disinterest from their primary caregivers, they adapt by suppressing their attachment system. They learn that expressing need or vulnerability doesn't lead to connection. It leads to shame, frustration, or indifference. To protect themselves, they build emotional walls.

In childhood, this looks like quiet self-sufficiency. In adulthood, it often manifests as emotional detachment, an over-focus on independence, and a discomfort with intimacy.

Core Beliefs of Avoidant Attachment:

- "I am alone and must take care of myself."
- "Needing others is weak or dangerous."
- "If I let someone get close, I will be engulfed or hurt."
- "To be safe, I must stay in control."

They don't think these things out loud. But their bodies know. Their nervous system has learned, "To stay safe, stay distanced." Their thermostat is too sensitive toward potential threat from intimacy. They always want to cool relationships when things feel too warm.

What Avoidant Attachment Looks Like
(and How to Heal)

DOMAIN	EXPRESSION	TRIGGER	DEFAULT REACTION	HEALING MOVE
Romantic Love	Withdrawal, low intimacy	Closeness, vulnerability	Shut down or pull away	Stay in the moment, express thoughts
Friendship	Surface-level, distant	Requests for emotional depth	Disengage	Practice small acts of openness
Parenting	Emotionally reserved	Child's distress	Discomfort, avoid	Validate feelings, mirror emotions
Work	Hyper-independence, overworking	Collaboration, feedback	Solo effort	Accept help, share responsibility
Faith/ Spirituality	Head over heart, performance-based	Relational language of grace	Detachment	Engage emotionally with God, not just ideas

The Nervous System & Avoidant Attachment

Avoidant attachment correlates with freeze, numbness, and emotional withdrawal. This can lead to a chronic shut-down of emotional response. They are internally calm but disconnected. Energy drops, emotional flatness sets in, and they feel fatigued. They can struggle to access feelings or emotions. Internally, they believe that feelings are not safe. They disconnect from their body and try to reason through everything. They are quick to say, "I'm fine," even in highly emotional situations.

In the Window of Tolerance, those with an avoidant pathway tend toward the hypo-aroused. They fail to bring the energy and engagement necessary to deal with the situation at hand.

The Shame Loop

While it looks like confidence (sometimes even pride), avoidant attachment is often driven by shame:

- "Why can't I feel more?"
- "Why do I keep pushing people away?"
- "Maybe I'm just cold or broken."

This shame is not loud. It's quiet, buried beneath layers of independence. Curt Thompson says, "Shame is not just a feeling. It's a neurobiological event. It's felt in the body long before it's processed in the mind."[13] Those with avoidant pathways often don't know they're lonely. They don't feel sad until the relationship ends. Then it all floods in, and they don't know what to do with it.

Those early memories of emotional rejection becomes internalized until we name it, hold it with compassion, and learn to choose differently.

PATH TOWARD SECURE ATTACHMENT

Healing avoidant attachment is not about becoming clingy or emotional. It's about becoming real. It's about allowing connection with self and others. It's about staying in it even when things feel too close.

As someone with anxious pathway learns they don't have to reach for another for regulation, someone with an avoidant pathway learns they can stay connected even when they are tempted to separate. They need to lean in when they want to run out.

Practices that Foster Growth:

PRACTICE	WHY IT HELPS
Mindful self-reflection	Builds awareness of internal emotional experience
Naming bodily sensations	Reconnects the mind with emotional states in the body
Therapy	Gently increases tolerance for emotional intimacy
Expressive journaling	Offers space to explore thoughts/feelings without judgment
Safe relationships	Practice staying when the instinct is to withdraw
Gradual vulnerability	Builds capacity to open up in layers

Key Insight: Healing doesn't mean becoming emotionally dependent. It means allowing yourself to be fully human—emotional, relational, and whole.

CLAIRE REVISITED

"If you need space, you can have it. But if you're pulling away, I'd encourage you to hang in there," Daniel tells Claire. And these days, she can actually hear it. It's neither pressure nor criticism; it's care.

Sometimes she feels smothered. She recognizes that she's pulling away, but both she and Daniel name it and navigate it.

When she gives her usual quick answer, "I'm fine," Daniel doesn't rush to fix her. He just waits. And sometimes, after a few moments of silence, Claire will say quietly, "Actually... I'm not fine." It's a small step, but a significant one.

She's learning to pause. To name what she feels. To trust that she won't fall apart just because she opened up. It's awkward sometimes. But she doesn't want to go back to who she used to be. Something has changed.

Claire is still herself, independent, capable, and steady. But now she's also honest. She's in love. And she's not afraid to say it. She feels safe with Daniel in a way she's never felt before.

Her independence no longer keeps her disconnected. Her capability isn't covering up her need. Her steadiness gives her the confidence to admit when she's not okay.

She looks back at her old patterns and sees them more clearly now. What she thought was control was actually fear. What she once saw as weakness—needing someone—she now sees as strength.

She hasn't changed overnight. Sometimes she still feels the

urge to run. But she doesn't always follow it. Now she knows other roads. And those new roads are leading somewhere better.

Healing the Three Fears

PATHWAY	FEAR	HEALING
Anxious	Being Abandoned	Soothe Self
Avoidant	Being Smothered	Stay Connected
Disorganized	Being Hurt	Sense Safety

DISORGANIZED ATTACHMENT:
THE FEAR OF BEING TRAUMATIZED (AGAIN)

IAN'S STORY

Ian doesn't remember one version of his parents. He remembers dozens.

His mom could be tender in the morning and passed out by dinner. His dad might be cheering from the sideline today and screaming at him tomorrow. Some nights, the house pulsed with laughter and music. Other nights, it was dead silent, so tense it felt dangerous.

Sometimes, Ian was left home alone, far too young to be by himself. But even when someone was there, it didn't mean he was safe.

By third grade, Ian had a system: scan the room, read the faces, adjust fast. And whatever you do, don't rock the boat.

But sometimes he couldn't help it. He'd get overwhelmed, cry, run to his parents... then pull away just as fast. He wanted comfort, but didn't trust it. He was an expert at disappearing. If the house felt explosive, he'd vanish. If someone spiraled, he'd show up.

His dad used to laugh when Ian tried to cheer him up. But

sometimes, those same efforts triggered a violent reaction. Ian never knew which version of his dad he'd get. So he walked a tightrope. And he got really good at cleaning up the mess afterward.

By high school, Ian had one rule: love and fear always come together. He longed for connection, but feared the people he loved most. So he didn't trust himself. He thought love might hurt people. That he might hurt people. When someone got close, *he* pushed them away. But when they pulled away, he panicked.

That pattern followed him into adulthood. He ghosted, cheated, raged, and ran. He's ended things before they started. He's stayed in relationships he never should've entered. The only thing he ever avoided was calm. Nothing made Ian more uncomfortable than peace. But chaos? Chaos felt like home.

More than once, Ian thought, *I'm just wired wrong. I ruin everything I touch.*

Then he met Elise.

At first, he couldn't believe she'd even talk to him. One date turned into two. And slowly, something started to build. But Ian waited for it to fall apart. Elise didn't play games. She didn't explode. She didn't vanish. She was steady.

When Ian pulled away, she didn't chase him or shame him. She waited. When he lashed out, she stayed calm, but clear. "I want to be close to you," she told him, "but it can't happen like this."

Ian had never known that love could be both safe and strong.

Elise still confuses him. But he's drawn to her, maybe because for the first time, love isn't something he has to manage or survive. It's something he can actually learn to trust.

And he's beginning to believe: maybe he isn't unlovable after all. Maybe the problem wasn't him. Maybe he just didn't know what real love looked like, until now.

What Is Disorganized Attachment?

Disorganized attachment arises when a child's caregivers are simultaneously a source of comfort and fear. This often stems from trauma, abuse, severe neglect, or chronic emotional unpredictability. The child learns that turning to the caregiver for safety might also expose them to harm.

The result is confusion. The brain wires itself for both proximity and protection, but when those impulses clash, it creates a nervous system in conflict. The child doesn't know whether to move toward or away from others. This unresolved tension continues into adulthood.

Core Beliefs of Disorganized Attachment:

- "I want to be close, but I don't feel safe."
- "Love is unpredictable and possibly dangerous."
- "If people knew the real me, they'd run."
- "I have to control others or be controlled."

Those with disorganized pathways may experience a mixture of anxious and avoidant behaviors, often flipping between them rapidly.

Disorganized Attachment Across Life Domains

DOMAIN	EXPRESSION	TRIGGER	DEFAULT REACTION	HEALING MOVE
Romantic Love	Hot-cold cycles, sabotage	Intimacy or perceived rejection	Cling or withdraw	Name feelings, ask for space without disappearing
Friendship	Inconsistency, mistrust	Vulnerability or conflict	Push away or test	Build predictable, low-stakes bonds
Parenting	Reactivity, shutdown, guilt	Child's emotions or stress	Collapse or overcontrol	Ground before responding, seek repair
Work	Inconsistent effort, resistance to feedback	Authority or visibility	Overwork or disengage	Build routine, self-regulation
Faith/ Spirituality	Extremes of passion and distance	Trust, intimacy with God	Idolize then avoid	Practice steady presence and rest

The Nervous System & Disorganized Attachment

Disorganized attachment often shows up in the body before it shows up in behavior.

People who experience this as their primary pathway live with a nervous system that can't find rhythm. They flip between panic and shutdown. In one moment their hearts race and hands shake. In the next moment, they go numb and silent. It can be characterized by a wide range of reactions: rage, anxiety, hypervigilance, numbness, dissociation, isolation, a quick flip from clingy panic to icy detachment, and an inability to stay grounded or consistent. The individuals often feel like they are living in survival mode, even when circumstances don't justify the level of threat they perceive.

The Shame Spiral

Disorganized attachment carries some of the deepest shame. Behaviors feel erratic even to themselves:

- "Why do I destroy the things I love?"
- "I can't trust anyone, not even myself."
- "I want a connection, but I'm terrible at it."

It's an exhausting loop, wanting closeness but fearing it, running toward intimacy and then away from it. And when the pattern repeats, the shame only grows.

It doesn't feel like a strategy. It feels like failure.

But that's not the whole story.

Daniels wrote, "Recognition that is met with curiosity and then compassion moves us toward integration."[14]

Healing doesn't come through guilt. It comes through kindness. When shame is met with understanding, not judgment, it starts to loosen its grip. The war inside us softens. And the fractured parts of us begin to come home. Those with disorganized attachment are not broken. They are fragmented, but thankfully, the fragments can be gathered.

Path Toward Secure Attachment

You don't heal disorganized attachment by thinking your way through it. You heal it by learning to feel safe again.

This isn't just about new ideas. It's about new experiences. It's the nervous system's work. It's relational repair. It's giving yourself what you never got: a safe place to be human.

Practices that Foster Growth:

PRACTICE	WHY IT HELPS
Somatic therapy	Calms the nervous system through breath, movement, and grounding
EMDR or trauma-focused therapy	Processes unresolved memories that drive reactivity
Safe relationships with firm boundaries	Rebuilds trust slowly and predictably
Self-talk and journaling	Separates present triggers from past trauma
Repairing ruptures	Replaces abandonment with connection and accountability

Key Insight: The goal is not to erase fear or dependence, but to bring both into balance through trust, awareness, and co-regulation.

A Reframed Narrative

Healing from disorganized attachment rarely comes all at once. It comes in moments.

Moments when someone notices the inner conflict and doesn't rush to fix it. Moments when they pause instead of panic. Moments when they say to themselves, "This part of me wants to be close. And this part is scared."

They begin to realize their contradictions aren't signs of failure; they're evidence of survival. They stop seeing intensity as brokenness. They stop assuming chaos disqualifies them from love. They begin to believe that connection doesn't have to come with pain.

Healing looks like staying when they would've run, speaking honestly instead of testing someone's patience, reaching for comfort and letting themselves receive it.

They start to trust that it's possible to feel safe and close. They learn that love doesn't always come with a catch. And slowly, they stop fearing peace.

It's not perfect. Some days, the old story still pulls hard. But now they know: it's not the truth. It's just a story.

And they're allowed to write a better one.

They're not stuck in survival mode anymore. They're choosing something new, one safe step at a time.

IAN REVISITED

Ian still wrestles with the shadows. There are days when Elise's kindness feels suspicious. Days when his body tenses before his mind catches up. Days when part of him wants to run, just to make sure he leaves her before she leaves him.

But now, he recognizes those temptations and quiets them in his mind. He no longer places them in the driver's seat of his life. His internal thermostat has learned to regulate properly.

In Elise, he's found something his childhood never offered. She's predictable, present, and loving. She's quick to own her mistakes, apologize, recognize Ian's feelings, and give space for his needs to be experienced and processed.

In himself, Ian discovers something even more surprising:

the ability to stay without sabotage. He hasn't destroyed this good thing that he has found. That's a first. While he still feels unworthy and unlovable at times, he's starting to recognize that he has some control over the outcomes he experiences.

He's listening. He's naming what's going on inside without feeling shame or expecting a harsh response. He's learning that love isn't supposed to be chaos. He's starting to find love as a place of rest.

Obviously, Ian hasn't healed everything. But he is building something new not just with Elise, but within himself. For the first time, he's realized that while his past has shaped him, it doesn't have to define him. Love doesn't have to hurt in order to be real.

CHAPTER 4:

ANXIOUS AND AVOIDANT IN RELATIONSHIPS

Zoe caught Ethan's eye on the first day of sophomore year. The school's computer system placed them in the same English class, and Ethan's quick decision-making led them to sit next to each other. For the entire fall semester, Ethan's favorite class was English. A good day was defined as a day in which he made Zoe laugh. A bad day was any day in which Zoe didn't give Ethan the attention he wanted. Most days were good days.

Although he couldn't verbalize it, Ethan was drawn to Zoe's emotions. She was full of such life. He never had to guess how she felt. She could cry, laugh, be afraid, or be happy without any hesitation. Deep down, Ethan wished he could do the same. But emotions weren't as easy with him.

At home, Ethan was well-loved. His dad was fiery, but Ethan knew how to navigate his quick temper. They shared a love for sports, and his dad coached him in every sport. His mom was always in the stands, keeping the scorebook for baseball, running the scoreboard for basketball, and cheering him on during track. Ethan assumed their family was like any other. Yet there were things he didn't know in high school that he could only see when looking back as an adult.

When Ethan was sad, his dad didn't know how to handle it. He wouldn't get mad at Ethan or shame him. He would simply disappear or push Ethan toward his mom. Emotions were things that men didn't show. When Ethan felt them, he learned that his mom was the safer option to deal with them. But in his mind, he thought he should grow out of those feelings and into true manhood. Self-dependence was the goal, and emotions were the threat to that desired outcome.

Yet that's what drew him to Zoe. She could express things he wanted to feel.

Zoe also came from a loving family. Her parents were divorced, but they always made sure she was well supported. In her mind, the divorce gave her more people to be loved by, and she was close with both step-parents. Internally, Zoe sometimes felt like her own personal rollercoaster. She was continually up and down. That's what drew her to Ethan. He seemed like a rock. He had the stability she desperately wanted.

That semester of English class led to dating for the rest of their high school years. Except for two days during their sophomore year of college, when Ethan lost his mind and broke up with Zoe before quickly getting back with her, the two have been together for 20 years and married for 15.

But they are in the counselor's office, unable to understand what is wrong. To the counselor, the issue is obvious.

Zoe has a primarily anxious pathway, which causes her to be extremely sensitive to any sense of abandonment. The slightest irregularity or movement causes her heart to race, and she feels the need to reach out to Ethan to ensure that they are still connected.

Ethan has a primarily avoidant pathway, which makes him extremely sensitive to any sense of suffocation. The slightest sense that another expectation or demand might be made of him causes his heart to race and causes him to feel the need to create space so that he can maintain his independence.

So, at any given moment, Zoe and Ethan are scanning their relationship on constant alert for their greatest fear: abandonment for Zoe and smothering for Ethan. The more unhealthy their connection, the more they both look for signs of danger, and the more they both find the signs (whether they are actually present or not).

Last week, something triggered one of them. It's not even clear who was triggered first. But Zoe felt like Ethan was pulling away, and Ethan felt like Zoe was trying to pull him close, so both kicked into survival mode.

Zoe reached out for a connection, but Ethan wanted space. So he took a metaphorical step away from her, which caused her anxiety to increase, which resulted in her pursuing Ethan with more vigor. This increased pursuit increased Ethan's fears, which caused him to flee with even greater speed.

Now, they are playing one-way chase. Ethan is trying to get away while Zoe is trying to connect. Looking back, this has been the pattern of the whole relationship. In high school, Ethan didn't want to go out every night, so some nights he would work late at his part-time job. This scared Zoe, which would cause her to dream up 100 scenarios of what might be wrong.

When texting became the norm, Zoe would rapid-fire text Ethan, making him even less likely to respond.

Sometimes the chase would last for a day, sometimes a week, and sometimes two weeks. But eventually, something would happen where they would both stop and reconnect. And when they did, they would have these assumptions:

> Zoe would think, "We have connected in a new way. We will forever be this close."

> Ethan would think, "I appeased her. I'll never have to do that again."

So, they would already be set up for the next fight: Zoe would inevitably be heartbroken that their deep connection isn't lasting forever, and Ethan would recognize that Zoe is no longer satisfied by last week's connection.

This is a typical pattern for couples who have primary or secondary patterns of anxious and avoidant attachment.

It sounds exhausting. When two people live out their non-secure patterns in a way that provokes one another toward a non-secure response, exhaustion is experienced by everyone (even their counselor).

The Push-Pull Dynamic

The most common relational dynamic involves at least one (often both spouses) having a primary secure pathway, but when that is not the case, it often results in one spouse leaning toward an anxious pathway and the other toward an avoidant pathway.

Like Ethan and Zoe, their non-secure tendency attracts them to the non-security in the other, but only because that non-security expresses itself in a different way. Two people with anxious patterns tend not to be drawn toward one another (they often find the other exhausting). And couples, where both spouses have primarily avoidant pathways tend not to last past the initial dating phase (because both attempt to avoid deeper intimacy).

But avoidant and anxious attract each other, offering the mirage of security, not realizing they are simply intermingling their same non-secure approaches to life and relationships.

When one spouse fears being abandoned and the other fears being smothered, a predictable pattern begins to unfold. We get sucked into the Infinity Loop.

The pattern doesn't begin with evil intent. It is simply two people doing what comes naturally. Zoe and Ethan's responses made perfect sense in their families of origin. Zoe needed to be on constant alert in her family to read the room, manage the emotions, and keep the peace. Ethan had no need to be on alert because emotions were not something to be valued or shared in his house. So he grew skeptical of others' emotions and ignorant of his own. These patterns are rooted in a fear that always dwells above the surface for Zoe and just below the surface for Ethan.

For Zoe, the fear is abandonment. She may not name it, but her body knows it. A delayed text, a distant tone, or an unmet expectation triggers her nervous system into high alert. Her brain interprets the distance as danger, and she responds by trying to bridge the gap. She wants reassurance, conversation, connection, a hug, an explanation, or anything to confirm that she is still safe.

For Ethan, the fear is engulfment or being smothered. He would never use those words, but when Zoe reaches for him in those moments of heightened need, he feels overwhelmed. He can barely meet her needs in the stress-free times, so the idea of having heightened expectations is too much. He doesn't feel pursued; he feels pressured. It's like he is the prize in a hunt. Zoe's intensity creates too high expectations. More demands and more responsibilities create added stress. He was okay when a relationship was a box to be checked, and Zoe was someone to be pursued. Once the ring was on her finger, he was ready to move on to the next adventure. Instead, he felt like he had become trapped in an endless barrage of expectations. So he desperately tries to pull away. He doesn't do so to hurt Zoe, but to protect himself. If she gets too close, he is certain he will fail.

Both of their thermostats are off. She too quickly heats things up and he too quickly cools things down. Neither are reading the room correctly. They don't recognize what is going on inside of themselves, much less what is going on in the other. So, their interpretations of each other are incorrect. Ethan thinks Zoe is trying to stifle him as a man. She's not. She desperately wants him to thrive as a man, in part, so that she will be safe. Zoe thinks Ethan is trying to hurt her. He's not. The last thing he wants to do is to hurt her. He wants Zoe to thrive, in part, so that she won't be as dependent on him to take care of her.

Yet they don't see these underlying motivations. Instead, Zoe interprets Ethan's distancing as the very abandonment she fears. Ethan interprets Zoe's pursuit as the very suffocation he dreads. Each partner's attempt to survive their internal panic unintentionally amplifies the panic of the other:

And so, the cycle begins:

1. **Zoe senses distance, so she pursues connection.**
2. **Ethan feels pressure, so he pulls away.**

3. Zoe panics, intensifying her pursuit.

4. Ethan flees further.

5. Both are hurt and neither feels understood.

6. They reconnect eventually, but with different assumptions:

- Zoe: "We're closer now. He understands me."

- Ethan: "We survived that. Please don't need that again soon."

They don't fight every moment, but tension simmers. Even during good seasons, both are watching. Waiting. On edge for the next round of misunderstanding, the next game of chase, the next push and pull.

Had they been wise, the couple would've sought help years ago. But instead, they endured. They assumed they just needed to love better, forgive, and figure it out. But what they needed was help to see their patterns, to understand why each of them did what they did, and to discover the true motivations under each other's actions.

They eventually reached out because they were exhausted. They've been exhausted. The whole process is exhausting. But finally, they couldn't take any more.

Both are convinced by a deep internal message:

- **For Zoe: "I am too much."**
- **For Ethan: "I am not enough."**

These messages lead to chronic misunderstanding. When we don't understand ourselves, we can't understand others. Conflict becomes cyclical. Small irritations are loaded with history. Over time, both partners begin to feel like failures. We are left to believe one of four negative options:

1. **As an individual, I'm broken.**
2. **My spouse is broken.**
3. **We are a bad match.**
4. **Marriage doesn't work.**

In most cases, none of those are true. Instead, we are engaged in a negative cycle because our unrecognized attachment patterns are dictating our actions and understandings.

When one spouse utilizes a non-secure pathway, the relationship can struggle. When both partners utilize a non-secure pathway, the worst-case scenarios for each are rehearsed and triggered daily. The partner with an anxious pathway gets an intermittent connection matching their family of origin. It's just enough to keep them hopeful, but not enough to feel secure. The partner with an avoidant pathway feels continually pressured and pursued. It's just enough to feel guilty, but not enough to feel free.

Without intervention, the cycle becomes self-reinforcing. Notice with Ethan and Zoe, their conclusions to the reconnection—her belief that it would be forever and his belief that he would never have to do that again—set them up for the next fight. Each keeps doing the only thing they know to experience agency and bonding, yet their actions lead to the opposite of the desired outcome. And the distance grows.

Here's another way the negative pattern can express itself.

The Table Illustration

Imagine a couple sitting at a dinner table having a romantic dinner. As the waiter approaches the table, he sees the woman's beautiful dress, jewelry, hair, and makeup. He sees the man's suit, wedding ring, hair, and smiling face. Yet there are things he can't see. Seated with legs under the table, half of their bodies are unseen to others. Half is seen and half is unseen.

Use this image as a way of understanding. When it comes to showing ourselves to others, we are divided in half—part is above the table, fully seen by others, and part is below the table, hidden and unseen.

One of the things below the table is our attachment needs. They are unseen but very present.

Consider Jill and Steve. You see him above the table, but he also has a lot going on below the table. You see her above the table; she is also just as much under the table.

Let's consider something that triggers a conflict between the two. The trigger could be anything. The specificity does not matter.

For this illustration, let's imagine that Jill walks into the kitchen and sees a sink overflowing with dishes. She looks over and sees Steve lying on the couch and watching a game. If those dishes trigger feelings of being unseen, unheard, unvalued, and unloved, she has a choice of how to surface those feelings (remember, feelings are below the table).

A secure approach would be to take a deep breath and

calmly, but assertively, tell Steve how she feels when she sees the dishes. "Honey, I know you work hard, and I love you for it. But when I've worked all day and come in and see these dishes in the sink, it makes me feel taken advantage of, undervalued, and somewhat like you think I'm your mother. I know you would never want that, so let's talk through what we can do."

That's a highly mature approach, but let's say Jill is tired, frustrated, and not working from a secure approach. Rather than surfacing her emotions, a non-secure approach would be to raise a protest.

PROTEST: A protest is an attempt to use one issue to get our spouse's attention about another issue—an unmet attachment need.

"I guess you don't care about these dishes," Jill says.

Notice the wording. She doesn't just talk about the issue—

the dishes–she raises the stakes of the conversation to be about Steve's heart, "I guess you don't care." Her protest is aimed at what's below the table for Steve, his heart.

Steve now has a choice. How does he respond? A secure response would be to ignore the metaphorical first punch and realize the protest isn't the real issue; the issue is what's going on below the table for Jill. He could say, "Help me understand what you feel when you see those dishes?"

But Steve doesn't respond securely. Instead, Jill's words said above the table are targeted at what Steve has going on below the table. And he feels attacked, shamed, and not enough. Rather than surfacing those emotions, "Let me start washing those dishes. And as I do, can I tell you how I feel when you imply that I don't care?" Steve responds to Jill's protest with a defense.

DEFENSE: A defense is an explanation focused on justifying oneself rather than recognizing the other's heart.

"I've been at work all day. I just sat down," Steve says.

Whether true or not, notice the problem with Steve's response; it's about himself. Jill's issue is her own unmet attachment needs. Rather than raising the actual issue, she made it about Steve's actions and ultimately his heart. Instead of seeing what the true issue is (Jill's heart) Steve defends himself and his actions.

Ironically, this makes Jill feel even more unseen, unheard, unvalued, and unloved.

So what does she do?

If the first protest didn't work, the only non-secure second step is to protest even harder. The first protest didn't get

Steve's attention, so she has to protest more.

"Well, you never seem to find the time to help out around the house," she says.

The first protest questioned his heart, but Jill's second protest was an all-defining failure of who Steve was, "... you never."

Of course, Steve should recognize the pattern and speak directly to Jill's heart rather than trying to defend his own. But he doesn't. His first defense didn't work, so he has one of two choices: up the ante on his defense or shut down.

Sadly, it doesn't matter which of these two he chooses. Both will have the same impact. Each will make Jill feel more unseen, unheard, unvalued, and unloved. Both greater defense and emotional shutdown fail to give Jill what she wants the most, for her heart to be seen.

Steve, afraid of saying the wrong thing, says nothing. He shuts down. This sends Jill into a panic. If her first protest didn't work and her even more intense protest didn't work, what must she do to get her heart seen? Steve's first defense didn't work, so he doesn't know how to respond without making things worse. But of course, this confirms Jill's previous statements, "...you never," and "...care."

The two get stuck in the Infinity Loop.

This pattern of protest and defense might happen consistently for a couple like Jill and Steve. It can just as easily switch roles when the topic is changed.

Imagine that Steve feels unseen, unheard, unvalued, and unloved. Rather than surfacing those feelings, he might protest.

"I thought we were going to have sex tonight," Steve says. Jill, rather than recognizing what's going on below the table for Steve, feels attacked, shamed, and not enough. She defends herself.

"We just did it two nights ago, wasn't that enough?" Jill responds.

Notice the response doesn't speak to Steve's heart, which tempts him to protest even harder.

"Well, I don't know if we are ever going to have sex again," he says.

Feeling more unworthy, Jill can either defend more strongly, "All you ever care about is sex," or shut down. Not wanting to say the wrong thing, she emotionally shuts down and goes to bed.

Once again, the couple is in the Infinity Loop even though the spouses have traded roles.

This is where many couples become stuck. Notice our natural tendency—to protest harder, defend more vigorously, or shut down—leads to the opposite outcome of what we desire. Rather than focusing on the real issue, both parties get distracted by the surface issue and litigate it while ignoring what's going on below the table.

The answer for both partners is to respond in a secure manner. And what is a secure response? It's to reveal what's below the table. As we model vulnerability for our spouse by exposing what is below the surface for us, we want to create a climate which woos the heart of our spouse out of hiding so they surface their emotions and desires.

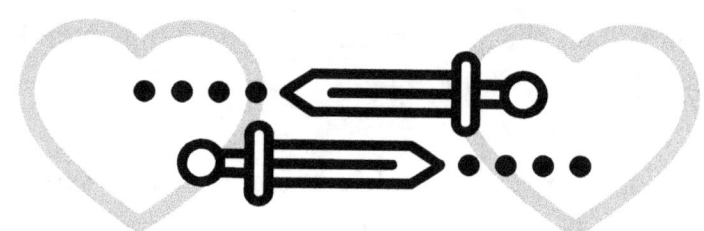

Notice what happens in the traditional Infinity Loop. Both spouses are using swords to pierce the heart of the other, all while claiming to simply stick to the issue at hand.

Instead, we need to place our hearts on the table and create a climate where our spouse feels safe enough to do the same. It's only when both hearts are on the table—surfaced to be seen—that true connection can take place.

This pattern explains why there are times when one issue can create a fight one night and result in nothing on another night. If my wife feels seen, heard, understood, loved, and appreciated, she can walk into a dirty kitchen, feel a sense of gratitude, put in her AirPods, and sing worship music while cleaning the dishes. Yet the next day she can walk in and see the same scene and think to herself, "I'm about to hurt somebody!" Why? Because if her attachment needs are unmet, the dishes trigger unmet needs and create a physical response within her. But if her attachment needs are fulfilled, the same trigger has little to no effect.

The Infinity Loop

When a couple argues the same way about different things, they've likely entered the Infinity Loop.

INFINITY LOOP: The Infinity Loop is a pattern of communication where both partners provoke the other by only dealing with what's above the table rather than compassionately dealing with what's below the table.

While nuances might be different for each couple, the underlying patterns are common across relationships. This is why what feels so unique to a couple is so predictable to a marriage counselor.

At the heart of the Infinity Loop are two actions: Protest and Defense. Both serve to distract from the real issue of what's going on below the table. Both cause each to focus on themselves rather than connecting with their spouse, which causes each to feel unseen, unheard, unvalued, and unloved.

Protest. Defense. Greater Protest. Greater Defense (or Shutdown). Repeat.

Notice, at no step along the way does either spouse stop and see the other. Instead, they both are driven deeper into their own unmet needs. And the disconnection continues.

The problem is the pattern. But the pattern often remains unseen, so each spouse doesn't understand the issue. In many situations, the partner with a more anxious pathway will frequently attribute the problem to their spouse. And in many situations, the person with the avoidant pathway sees themselves as the problem. Ironically, many couples agree on who the problem is. But they are wrong. The issue isn't the person; it's the pattern.

Until the pattern is recognized, the couple will remain stuck in an increasing sense of hopelessness.

Hope comes as a couple learns the pattern. This empowers them to recognize what is going on within themselves and to better interpret what their spouse is experiencing.

> The Protestor isn't trying to be critical.
> They just want to be seen

The Defender isn't trying to be dismissive.
They just want to be safe.

Neither understands how to say that directly.

Thankfully, there is a way out. It's found as we stop trying to win the argument and start trying to understand what's going on below the surface.

What's Going On Below the Table?

In every relationship, what is said and seen are only half the story. The far more important half is what is felt, but unspoken, present, but unseen.

Our attachment needs live below the table.

When a couple like Jill and Steve get stuck in protest or

defense, they are arguing about what's above the table–the dishes, tone of voice, texting patterns, intimacy rhythms, parenting, visiting in-laws, etc. But the real issue drives the emotional tone of the conversation, and it's under the table.

Let's look at each below the table.

Jill's Under-the-Table Story (Anxious Pathway):

When Steve pulls away (or even when Jill perceives he might), Jill's nervous system flares. Her body remembers all the times when emotional connection felt uncertain. She doesn't consciously think, "He's abandoning me," but her body responds as though it is happening. Her thermostat tries to regulate a temperature that hasn't actually changed.

What she's really wondering is:

- **"Do you still love me?"**
- **"Do I matter to you?"**
- **"Are you still with me in this?"**
- **"Are you going to leave me?"**

But instead of saying those things, she protests.

Above the table: frustration.

Below the table: fear.

Steve's Under-the-Table Story (Avoidant Pathway):

When Jill intensifies her pursuit, Steve's nervous system tightens. His body learned long ago that strong emotion is overwhelming and unsafe. He fears he won't handle things correctly. He will say the wrong thing, disappoint her again, or lose the space he needs to feel okay.

What he really wants to know is:

- "Am I enough? Will I ever be?"
- "Will you still love me when I fail to fix this?"
- "Can you accept me even if I don't know what to say?"
- "Can I be close without being consumed?"

But instead of surfacing those fears, he defends:

Above the table: logic.

Below the table: fear.

The Irony

Interestingly, both Jill and Steve feel very similar. Both want to feel safe, be seen, and connect. But because neither knows how to surface their heart, they end up attacking the very thing they are trying to protect.

Jill's protest feels like criticism to Steve.

Steve's withdrawal feels like abandonment to Jill.

They both see what they are looking for, even when it isn't necessarily there.

Both are trying to avoid pain, yet both are increasing it. The longer this goes on, the harder it becomes to understand what is real and what is projected. With both partners looking for negative things, they are quick to find them.

Harm or Health?

Imagine you and someone significant in your life sitting across the table. Both of you are hiding your hearts. You hold them in your hands, in your lap. Those hearts are tender, full of hurts, and have a long history of pain.

non-secure approaches create the very outcome we are trying to avoid.

You desperately want to show your heart to the other, but you are afraid.

If your spouse has the courage to put their heart on the table, are you certain that you will treat it right? Notice the question. I didn't ask, will you intend to treat it right? Intention matters, but actions do as well.

Unless we have done the work to understand ourselves

and to better know our spouse, we cannot ensure that we will treat them right. As a matter of fact, we can almost guarantee that on many occasions we will treat them wrong. Not because of poor intention but because we lack the skill and self-awareness to focus on them rather than defend ourselves.

Non-secure attachment prevents us from consistently treating others' hearts well because we don't know how to care for our own hearts properly.

A Pathway Forward

If couples like Jill and Steve want to stop the cycle of disconnection, they don't just need more information. They need new habits. The goal isn't to fight better. It's to relate in a different way with themselves and each other. Here's a three-part pattern to change: pause the protest, drop the defense, and surface the heart.

1. Pause the Protest

Every person will have to protest. Things happen that we don't like or understand, and we need to vocalize those things so we can handle them and move forward. Dishes need to be done. Children need to be disciplined. Bills need to be paid.

But we should pause the protest, so we can first have introspection to make sure the protest we are about to raise is the actual issue and is raised in a fair/respectful manner. It's fine to bring up the dirty sink, but we first ought to make sure the issue is the sink and not the feelings of being unseen or undervalued.

Pausing the protest means creating space between the feeling and the reaction. It means asking:

"What's really going on beneath this irritation?"

"What do I actually need right now?"

"What's the primary (not secondary) issue?"

Too often, we protest over a secondary issue. It matters. And it should be addressed. But we put the primary emotion with the secondary issue, and this confuses us and others.

It's easy to recognize in others. When I'm speaking with a couple and one person's emotional response doesn't match the situation, I know something else is at play. When their emotional response reaches an eight, but the issue is a minor inconvenience, it's clear that something greater is fueling all that emotional energy.

Pausing the protest helps us discover if there's more to it. It also empowers us to protest in a proper way. Accusation, escalation, and contempt are not useful ways to get our spouse to positively respond. But they are tools we often use when trying to raise a secondary issue when we are actually upset about a primary issue.

2. Drop the Defense

Defensiveness is instinctive. When we feel accused, we explain. When we feel cornered, we justify. But defenses rarely restore connection.

Either the secondary issue is truly the real concern, or it's simply the channel through which authentic, underlying emotions can surface, and the primary issue at play is that our spouse feels unseen, unheard, and undervalued. At that point, our defense puts the focus on us, making them feel even more unseen, etc.

If the issue being protested actually is the main concern, then we need to be practical about how to solve the problem, rather than defending our previous actions.

So, defenses often reinforce the very disconnection we're trying to escape. Dropping the defense means listening to what your spouse is really saying. It looks beyond their words and tries to locate their wounds. It means resisting the urge to explain, correct, or escape. It means pointing the spotlight back on their deepest concerns, empathizing, and trying to understand what they truly need.

A great response could be, "Before I defend myself, let me try to understand you."

When defenses fall, empathy can rise.

3. Surface the Heart

Once we pause the protest and drop the defense, we are freed to do something more vital: surface the heart.

This process is twofold: It means having the vulnerability to put our heart on the table, and it means creating a climate where our spouse feels safe to do the same.

Both are unique skills. Yet as we learn one, we become better at the other.

To surface the heart is to say:

- **"Here's what's going on inside of me."**
- **"Here's what I'm afraid of."**
- **"I don't know how to say this, but I'm going to try."**

Surfacing our heart means having the awareness to know what we are feeling and the courage to bring it to the table rather than being distracted by secondary issues.

Creating a climate where our spouse can reveal their heart means we will encourage and nurture their vulnerability rather than stifling it. The primary tool for this is to stay curious about them rather than feeling defensive about us.

We might say:

- "Tell me more."
- "What was that like for you?"
- "I'm listening."
- "I can see how you would feel that way."
- "Thank you for telling me that."

When couples practice this together, the temperature in the relationship shifts. The partner with a more anxious pathway learns how to soothe themselves and knows they don't have to chase their partner. The partner with the more avoidant pathway learns they don't have to hide. They can lean in when they are tempted to step away. Both feel safer.

This is the practice of love. It's not performance. It's the desire to live up to the vows we committed to each other. It's learning to feel appropriate fear but not be driven by it.

6 Questions to Invite Our Spouse's Heart to the Surface:

1. What's been on your heart lately that I may have missed?

2. What's something you've wanted to tell me but weren't sure how or didn't know how I would respond?

3. Is there anything that you've been carrying alone that you want me to carry with you?

4. I want to know you better. Can you help me? I'd like to understand this from your side?

5. If you had a magic wand and could create our future, what would it look like?

6. When have you felt most seen, heard, valued, and loved in the last month? When have you felt the opposite?

10 Statements that Tell Your Spouse to Keep Their Heart Concealed:

1. You're overreacting.

2. Don't be so emotional.

3. Calm down.

4. That's not what happened.

5. Here we go again.

6. You always/You never.

7. You shouldn't feel that way.

8. You're being too sensitive.

9. There's nothing you can say to change my mind.

10. I don't have time for this.

A New Way Forward for Steve, Jill, and You

"You're not broken," the counselor said. "You are both afraid. Each of you have developed different strategies to be safe, and neither is working."

For years, Steve and Jill had seen themselves as failures. At times they blamed each other, at other times they blamed themselves, and sometimes they just thought they were cursed. But the whole time, they were tired.

Now they are healing. They know they are not unique. Their problems are not unusual. The counselor hadn't screamed and left the room when they talked about their issues. Instead, it was like she could nearly finish their sentences.

"You clearly love each other," she said. "You just haven't learned how to fully show that love to yourself or one another. That's what we can fix."

For the next three months, the counselor walked Steve and Jill through a process of discovery. Yes, they had to look at their family of origins and recognize neither was perfect. They discovered their non-secure pathways. Their primary fixation wasn't about their failings. It was about learning secure attachment. To the extent that they could understand what a secure response was and grow in the ability to respond securely no matter what they were feeling, their relationship would change.

CHAPTER 5:

LEARNED (EARNED) SECURE ATTACHMENT:
LIVING IN TRUST

Whether one knows about Attachment Theory or is learning for the first time, readers can now be divided primarily into two categories. Some will identify with secure attachment and see that it is their primary pathway. While they likely can see some non-secure tendencies in their relationships, their challenge is to lean more into what comes naturally to them and choose the secure way.

But others have now been given language that explains much of their lives and some of their past relationship struggles. They now recognize their primary pathway is non-secure. Whether it's anxious, avoidant, or disorganized, matters less than the fact that they've been utilizing non-secure approaches, which have often thwarted the very outcomes they've desired.

The way we love today results from how we were loved yesterday. But the way we will love tomorrow results from how we choose to love today.

If the book ended here, those with primarily non-secure pathways (including the author) would feel stuck.

But there is good news. While we didn't choose the pathways we learned early in childhood, we do get to choose the way forward.

Remember, non-secure attachments are pathways, not identities. It's what we sometimes do, not who we are. We are not enslaved to our patterns, unable to make changes.

You are not stuck.

Attachment is adaptive. That means it can change. For those of us who didn't start with secure attachment, we can grow into it. This is what psychologists call Earned Secure Attachment or Learned Secure Attachment.[15]

Earned security means that through intentional work, you can reshape your primary ways of connecting, trusting, and loving. You can develop new patterns that support vulnerability, safety, and resilience.

Growing up in Arkansas, we would take an old two-lane highway to get from my hometown to the University of Arkansas to watch the Hogs play football. But when I was in high school, a new divided highway was built, requiring a crew to blast through a mountain to create a tunnel. I'll never forget the first time I drove the new road. What had been a 90-minute journey through winding mountains became a straight shot at a high rate of speed. It cut the drive time in half.

In many ways, creating an earned security feels like this. It's a lot of work, like blasting through a mountain. It takes a good amount of time; roads aren't built in a day.

Yet when the work is complete, you can't imagine living any other way.

What Is Earned (Learned) Secure Attachment?

Earned secure attachment refers to the process by which someone who did not grow up with consistent emotional safety and connection learns, over time, to develop secure ways of relating. It's called "earned" or "learned" because it's not developed in the formative first few years of life but is chosen through intentional healing and repeated experiences of relational trust.

Non-secure attachment (anxious, avoidant, or disorganized) forms in childhood when caregivers are inconsistent, unavailable, unpredictable, overly controlling, absent, or frightening. These early patterns become internal templates. They become the interpretive tool we use on others and on relationships. They define how we expect others to behave, how we regulate our emotions, and how we protect ourselves from pain.

But attachment is not destiny. Our brains and our bodies are capable of being rewired. Because of neuroplasticity, new experiences can change the pathways in our mind. That's where earned secure attachment begins.

Core Features of Earned Secure Attachment:

1. **The past informs you but doesn't own you.**
   Earned security doesn't require us to understand everything about our upbringing, but understanding some basic ways we were impacted is a prerequisite. Why we do what we do is an interpretive key that helps us change behaviors.

2. You pause before you react.

Non-secure attachment is our autopilot.
Without thought, we respond, especially in times
of stress, in a non-secure way. To change, we
must stop reacting and start reflecting. As we
reflect, we can better understand ourselves and
others. That allows us to choose the secure
response.

3. You get curious instead of critical.

Change is inhibited by judgment. When we judge
ourselves and others, we remain stuck in rigid or
chaotic structures. As we grow curious, we can
see beyond the surface explanations and to the
causes behind our (and others') actions.

4. You take the risk to be real.

Non-secure attachment is an adaptive strategy to protect ourselves. Learned secure attachment allows us to let our guard down and connect with ourselves and others.

5. You can settle yourself and be settled by others.

Someone with primary anxious pathways overly depends on others to soothe them, lacking any ability to soothe themselves. Someone with an avoidant pathway overvalues self-reliance and cannot lean on others. Learned security allows us to do both.

6. You know how to repair after a conflict.

Secure attachment doesn't mean less conflict; it means the ability to better repair after conflict in a way that deepens the connection.

How Do We Develop Earned Security?

Reading this book will not create secure attachment. It can be the catalyst, but reading about or understanding the concepts, can't produce results. Why? Because secure attachment is not simply the byproduct of knowing what it is. It requires more of us. Knowing matters, but ultimately, meeting attachment needs is something we feel, more than we know.

There isn't an exact formula for developing earned security. It's important to recognize it's a process. As I have developed an earned security with my wife, and it now extends to other relationships, there are still moments and situations where I quickly revert to old mindsets and thoughts, especially during times of stress or weariness. The old pathways will always be in our brain and will always be available to us. The difference is we have new choices, and even when we make old choices, we can recognize them and change, one intentional step at a time.

Here are four key practices that lead to earned security:

1. Grow in Self-Awareness: Know Your Pattern

You cannot change what you do not notice.

The first step toward earned security is identifying your default attachment response. Are you anxious, scanning for signs of rejection and pursuing connection out of fear? Are you avoidant, minimizing emotions and retreating to regain control? Or are you disorganized, flipping between extremes, and struggling to find consistency?

Learn to observe your reactions without shame. Ask:

- "What do I feel when someone gets emotionally close?"
- "How do I typically react when I feel hurt or unseen?"
- "What does 'safety' look like in a relationship to me?"

Awareness turns unconscious patterns into conscious choices. Once you can see the loop, you can begin to step out of it.

2. Widen Your Window of Tolerance
(Grow Your Ability to Stay Present)

Attachment wounds are stored not just in your mind, but also in your body.

When you're triggered, your nervous system reacts automatically. The body of an anxiously attached person is more likely to move into panic: racing heart, shallow breath, impulsive speech. The body of an avoidant person pulls inward: numbness, shutdown, detachment. The body of someone with disorganized attachment may freeze or shift quickly between both states.

The window of tolerance is the space between total shutdown and emotional overwhelm.

To earn secure attachment, you must grow what Siegel calls your window of tolerance.[16]

Those with non-secure attachment tend to have a narrow window of tolerance. Conditions have to be just right in order for them to feel calm and safe. Yet those with earned secure attachment can not only widen their window of tolerance, but they can also better recognize when they are at the edges of that window.

The goal isn't to avoid triggers. It's to become skilled at staying present when they happen. It's learning our bodies so well that we can hear what they're telling us and then lead them to a place of peace and calm, even when circumstances around us pull us toward rigidity or chaos.

3. Practice Vulnerability:
Speak from Your Heart, Not From Your Wound

Most of us learned to protect ourselves from pain by performing, pleasing, withdrawing, blaming, or minimizing. But those protections keep us from connection. Earned security develops when we begin openly expressing our true emotions instead of hiding behind protests and defenses. It involves assertive (not passive or aggressive) communication. Express emotions directly, don't just hint at them.

Instead of:

- "You never listen to me."
  Try: "I feel alone and afraid that I don't matter."

- "Whatever, just forget it."
  Try: "I want to talk about this, but I'm afraid I'll be misunderstood."

- "Why do I always have to ask for help?"
  Try: "It would mean a lot to me if you noticed what I need and offered to help without my asking."

Speaking vulnerably does not guarantee your partner will respond well, but it gives them the *chance* to. It also shifts your brain and body toward integration.

4. Nourish Safe Relationships That Reinforce New Patterns (Let The Right People In)

No one earns secure attachment alone. We heal in relationships. This doesn't mean perfect relationships.

It means consistent, present, and attuned relationships where:

- Emotions are met with respectful curiosity, not shame
- Conflict ends with repair, not silence
- There's freedom to be honest without fear of rejection

For many, this comes through:

- A secure spouse who models safety over time
- A wise therapist who listens without judgment
- A faithful friend who stays steady even when you're struggling
- A healthy spiritual relationship with God that reshapes identity and worth

Every time someone meets your heart with gentleness instead of harm, your nervous system learns: *It's okay to be seen. I am not in danger here.*

How We Grow Into Earned Secure Attachment

PRACTICE	WHAT IT BUILDS	WHY IT MATTERS
Self-Awareness	Noticing your patterns	So you can respond instead of react
Window of Tolerance	Staying calm in the hard moments	So you don't shutdown or blow up
Practicing Vulnerability	Naming what's true instead of hiding behind defenses	So connection becomes possible again
Safe Relationships	Rewiring through consistent love or fear of loss	So trust becomes your new normal

The process of earning security is not about pretending to be different. It's about slowly becoming someone who no longer lives from fear because you've learned how to be safe, even in conflict, and loved, even in your imperfection.

How Couples Can Grow Secure Together

Attachment Theory is built on relationships. The human brain needs others to reflect and clarify who we are. This is why solitary confinement is so grueling. It's why abandonment is so traumatic. We are individual people, but we can't truly be individual without finding our place in a community.

So, we cannot learn secure attachment on our own. We need others. Romantic relationships can be a powerful force that create a secure attachment within us. On one hand, they can be the most difficult because no relationship triggers our attachment behavior system like intimate relationships, but these connections also can provide the climate (love) and conditions (lots of opportunity) to grow into secure attachment.

The greatest wounds in our lives were caused when people were supposed to love us well but didn't. (Remember, that's not necessarily a failure of intent. It's often a failure of skill or opportunity.) Yet we are most often healed as God pours his love through someone who didn't have to love us, but chose to do so. We can be that for our spouse, and our spouse can be that for us.

And it doesn't require one to have a primarily secure pathway. Although that makes it easier, even if both spouses have primarily non-secure pathways (often one anxious and one avoidant), they can learn together how to create a secure relationship.

Here are four actions we can take to offer our spouse a climate where they can develop a more secure pattern:

1. Be a Safe Base and a Safe Haven

Imagine your spouse wants to start a new business or go back to school. A secure partner cheers them on while remaining emotionally present when the stress is high.

A safe base provides stability, allowing our spouse to launch from us and explore, grow, and express their individuality.

A safe haven is the place they return to for comfort, reassurance, and emotional shelter.

Both are necessary. And both occur as we learn what it means to provide safety for our spouse. Notice, this combination values both their agency and your connection. It demonstrates the two are not at odds, but rather complement one another. In non-secure attachment, we feel like we have a false choice: I can either be me or I can be in a relationship. In secure attachment, we learn we can be both.

Consider the power of these expressions:

- "I love seeing you do something that brings you to life."
- "I'm grateful that you have great friends."
- "You're safe here. You don't have to hold it together."
- "Take the space you need. I'm not going anywhere."

Security comes not from a perfect connection, but from knowing *I can come back and you'll still be here.*

2. Stay Present During Activation

When your spouse's attachment system is activated, they will likely behave in ways that are rooted in fear: anxiety, anger, shutdown, avoidance. The temptation will be to match their energy by either escalating or retreating. But remember, the answer to anxious or avoidant attachment is not the opposite non-secure approach. The answer is always the secure response. If you can stay present and secure when your spouse is activated, it can go a long way to helping them grow.

To help your spouse move toward secure attachment:

- Regulate yourself.
- Avoid personalizing their dysregulation.
- Use gentle words to remind them they're not alone:
    - "I can tell you're hurting. I want to understand."
    - "We don't have to solve this right now; I just want to stay close."
    - "Let's take a break and try again when we both feel calmer."

Your presence trains their nervous system to stay present, too. The longer you both stay in the room (emotionally and physically), the more healing becomes possible. (Note: there are times to leave a room. If you need space to emotionally regulate, it's acceptable to leave the room for a stated period of time. But you must come back or your spouse will feel abandoned.)

3. Name the Pattern (Not the Person)

Human beings are far more complex than a simple label, especially a label of attachment. While we do have patterns and pathways, it is not helpful to define the totality of who we are (or our spouse is) by an attachment style. I'm not anxiously attached. I have a primary anxious pathway. But I also have many secure relationships, while I can also act in avoidant ways at times. I'm far more than a label. And the danger of a label is when I label myself, it can become self-fulfilling and self-justifying. When others label me, they can read into situations and scenarios information that isn't true.

We shouldn't label others. However, it is useful for identifying actions and labeling patterns. I will often say to myself, "That is an anxious approach." This self-talk reminds me I have a choice regarding a secure pathway. And it's very helpful to identify the negative cycle in your and your partner's relationship.

When we name the pattern (and not the person), it externalizes the problem and allows spouses to get on the same side to fight the pattern rather than each other.

So instead of saying:

- **"You are so anxious."**
- **"You always shut down."**
- **"Don't get so emotional."**

Say:

- "This feels like that loop we get stuck in where you get quiet and I get louder."

- "I don't want us to fall back into that protest-and-defend dynamic again."

- "What's going on under the table right now for both of us?"

By shifting the focus from blame to pattern, you become collaborators rather than combatants. The goal isn't to fix each other; it's to notice what's happening and choose something new.

4. Celebrate Progress, Not Perfection

Change is a process. Perfection is never the goal because it's not realistic. No couple perfectly handles conflict, change, or each other. Perfection isn't possible, but progress is. Everyone can change. Celebrating every improvement energizes the transformation.

Setbacks are inevitable, but over time, even how we handle setbacks changes. A common pattern is that after learning about Attachment Theory, we can look back and see our mistakes. Then we get to where we can notice our pattern after it happens. Then we start noticing it in the middle. Eventually, we can recognize what is about to happen and change it before it does.

Healing isn't linear. One day, you will make great progress, and it will feel like things will forever be different. The next day, you will revert to old patterns and feel like nothing has changed. That's normal. The focus is on what direction you're headed.

Name the progress when it happens. See it in yourself and say it about your spouse:

- "Thank you for staying present during that conversation. I know it couldn't have been easy."

- "I noticed you paused before reacting. I see your effort."

- "That felt different in how we have often handled things. I'm proud of us."

Just like the negative cycle can adversely rewire our brains, positive reinforcement can also rewire them. Visible progress changes the climate in our minds and in our marriage.

How Couples Help Each Other Earn Secure Attachment

PRACTICE	WHAT IT DOES
Safe Base / Safe Haven	Grounds the relationship in trust
Stay Present During Activation	Regulates the nervous system in real time
Name the Pattern, Not the Person	Creates a shared language for healing
Celebrate Progress	Builds momentum and reduces shame

Signs You Are Experiencing Earned Secure Attachment

Because change is a process, it takes time. Secure attachment doesn't just suddenly appear one day and then forever define your relationship. It took me ten years before I learned that I could tell my wife I didn't like something she would cook. Ten years until I felt comfortable. But that was before I knew about Attachment Theory. I was growing into secure attachment simply because of Jenny's consistent love.

Notice: In a healthy marriage, love is contagious. A spouse who has a secure presence can instill security in someone who has never known it. However, the opposite is also true. If the relationship is unhealthy, even a secure spouse can start to lose their footing.

Love has the power to change. Love wedded to knowledge has the power to change even faster.

Here are some practical signs that earned secure attachment is starting to appear:

Relational Signs

- You can stay emotionally present during conflict without shutting down or exploding.

- You express needs calmly and directly, without guilt or manipulation.

- You feel comfortable being alone, but also enjoy closeness without fear of losing yourself.

- You and your spouse can repair conflicts more quickly and with less damage.

- You can tolerate temporary disconnection without spiraling into panic or withdrawal.

Emotional Signs

- You feel more curious than defensive when your spouse is upset.

- You don't take everything personally.

- You recognize that your feelings are valid, but not always accurate.

- You experience a greater sense of internal calm, even during disagreement.

- You feel more confident in your worth, even when things are messy.

Spiritual and Identity Signs

- You no longer view yourself through the lens of your past pain.

- You trust that you are loved, even when you're not performing.

- You feel more capable of giving grace and receiving it.

- You don't fear vulnerability as weakness; you begin to see it as strength.

A Visual Summary

OLD PATTERN	EARNED SECURE SHIFT
Reacting from fear	Responding from grounded presence
Protesting or defending	Naming emotions with clarity and care
Avoiding difficult conversations	Engaging with honesty and curiosity
Feeling hijacked by emotion	Managing emotions without shutting down
Assuming disconnection is permanent	Trusting the relationship can recover

Earned Secure Love Over Just Surviving

For a lot of couples, survival is the goal. Marriage is more difficult than they predicted, and they are simply trying to navigate day-to-day life. While lasting marriage is noble, I want a higher goal for couples. What if, instead of surviving, they were able to discover a secure love?

We can't deny the impact the early years of life have on us. We are greatly shaped by our family of origin and how our initial needs were met. Yet we aren't enslaved to our first experiences. Each of us can take responsibility for our lives and change the way we love. Non-secure pathways can be transformed.

Secure love isn't perfect. It still includes disagreements, hard seasons, and emotional turmoil. But it's marked by resilience and built by repair. It's safe and honest. The stability of a secure attachment stands in stark contrast to the struggles of non-secure connections.

Couples who move toward secure attachment over time experience:

- A shared language for emotional safety
- Quicker recovery from conflict
- More space for individuality without fear of abandonment
- Deeper joy in connection that doesn't require control
- A relationship that becomes a place of refuge, not tension.

When security is earned, love becomes a place you can rest, not perform. You no longer have to hide parts of yourself or protect your heart with protest or withdrawal. You can bring your full self to the table. And you can trust your partner to do the same.

CHAPTER 6:

THE BIBLICAL BACKGROUND OF ATTACHMENT THEORY

Attachment Theory didn't start in the church. It came from psychology. But it tells a story that the church has told all along: something broke in Genesis 3, when sin entered the scene.

Instead of perfect children born to perfect parents being raised with entirely secure love, sin was introduced to both sides of the equation.

Being a child became much more challenging—being raised by sinful parents isn't nearly as easy as being raised by perfect people. And parenting changed significantly— raising perfect children is much simpler than raising children with a sinful nature.

Attachment theory explains the differences between the two.

Here's a Biblical overview:

We were made for secure love. God's original desire was for Adam and Eve to walk with God in perfect intimacy and trust. No fear. No shame. No hiding. Genesis 2:25 captures it perfectly, "The man and his wife were both naked, and they felt no shame."

That is the very essence of secure attachment: complete

vulnerability with no fear of rejection. Both individuals are seen, known, valued, and loved. Both have a total sense of self while being completely bonded with one another and God.

But Genesis 3 changes everything.

When sin enters the world, it brings with it fear. When Adam and Eve eat from the tree, their first response is not repentance; it is panic. They don't run to God. They hide from Him. They don't protect each other. They shame and blame each other. Genesis 3:10, "I was afraid...so I hid."

Life after the fall is defined by fear, shame, blame, and hiding. All are enemies to secure attachment. All lead us to the adaptations of non-secure attachment.

Imagine if the fall had never happened. There would be no

fear of rejection, no neglect, no criticism, and no emotional shutdowns. Children would be thoroughly delighted in and always delightful. They would be emotionally mirrored, giving them a sense of connection and self. Marriages would be full of grace and connection. Communities and neighborhoods would be safe and healthy.

Secure attachment would be universal.

But that is not our world.

Instead, every parent since Eden has passed on, to some degree, their broken patterns of relating. Not because they're evil, but because they're human. As David confessed in Psalm 51:5, "Surely I was sinful at birth, sinful from the time my mother conceived me."

We are born not just into a world of sin, but into

relationships shaped by sin. Parents are impacted by fear, insecurity, and unhealed wounds. As a result, we grow up with attachment patterns that reflect far more of Genesis 3 than Genesis 2.

Attachment Styles as Echoes of the Fall

- **Anxious Attachment** echoes Eve's longing for connection and fear of abandonment. (Gen. 3.16) It says, "Do you still want me? Am I enough?"

- **Avoidant Attachment** echoes Adam's withdrawal and self-justification. (Gen. 3.10) It says, "If I stay too close, I'll be exposed."

- **Disorganized Attachment** echoes both pushing and pulling in panic. (Gen. 4.8) "I need love, but I don't trust it won't hurt me."

Non-secure attachment patterns are strategies developed in a fallen world to protect ourselves from being hurt again. Yet they often simply add to the hurt. Actions and responses that helped in the past, hurt in the present.

Thankfully, the Gospel offers a different way. We can identify, understand, and replace our non-secure attachment styles with healthier ones. We are not stuck in old habits; we can learn new ways to connect and love. That is one of the gifts of the Gospel.

God's Response: A Pursuing, Secure Love

What does God do in Genesis 3?

He pursues. "But the Lord God called to the man, "'Where are you?'" (Genesis 3:9)

He doesn't abandon Adam and Eve. He seeks them out. He covers their shame. And He sets in motion a plan for restoration.

In attachment terms, God models secure love:

- He *pursues,* even when they hide.
- He *names the rupture* but doesn't withdraw.
- He *provides,* even after consequences are declared.
- He *remains* emotionally and relationally available.

Throughout Scripture, we see this pattern again and again. God remains a secure base and safe haven for His people.

Jesus: The Embodiment of Secure Attachment

In Jesus, we see what it looks like to live with a completely secure attachment to the Father. He is:

- **Non-defensive when accused (1 Peter 2:23)**
- **Emotionally honest in grief (John 11:35)**
- **Assertive without aggression (John 8:46)**
- **Dependent without shame (John 5:19)**
- **Capable of both intimacy and solitude (Mark 1:35)**
- **Fully individual, yet completely connected (John 10:30)**

And Jesus offers to extend that same secure connection to us: "Remain in me, as I also remain in you." (John 15:4)

This is the Gospel invitation, not just to be saved from the consequences of sin, but to be restored to a secure relationship with God, with others, and even with ourselves.

The Church: A Community of Earned Secure Attachment

In a fallen world, we rarely receive perfect love from our parents, but we can experience healing love in community.

The local church, when healthy, becomes the context for earned secure attachment:

- **Safe people who show up consistently (Hebrews 10:24-25)**
- **Spiritual leaders who mirror God's compassion (1 Peter 5:2-3)**
- **Vulnerable friendships marked by grace (James 5:16)**
- **Honest conflict followed by forgiveness and repair (Colossians 3:13)**

When Christians live out the fruit of the Spirit—love, joy, peace, patience, kindness, goodness, faithfulness, gentleness, self-control—they aren't just being moral. They are living with secure attachment.

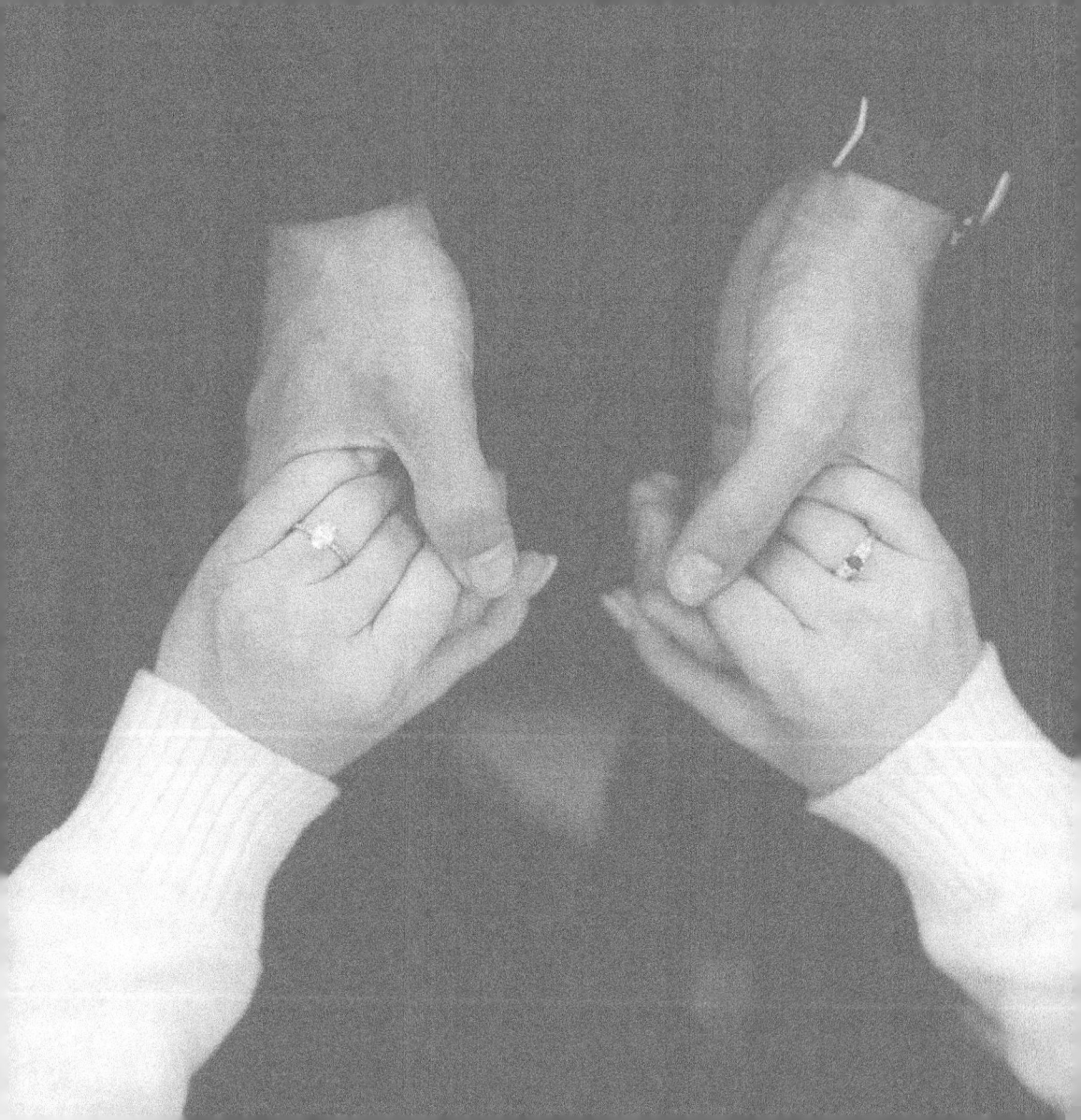

CONCLUSION

Remember the opening story to the book about Jason, Emily, and their old thermostat?

Buried behind a wall, it had been quietly trying to regulate a room it could no longer read. That forgotten device, wired into their system, continued to send signals based on inaccurate data.

Once they found it and removed it, things began to improve. However, they soon realized that merely identifying the old system wasn't enough. For true comfort, they needed a new thermostat. One that could read the room accurately and respond wisely.

Of course, even the new system isn't perfect. Sometimes the battery dies. Sometimes Jason turns the AC down while Emily wants it up. Life still gets out of sync. But now they know what's happening. They are no longer ruled by a hidden force shaping their relationship from the background.

That's the invitation of this book—not to find perfection, but to find freedom. When we understand how our past has shaped us, we can begin to choose a new way of loving. That's the opportunity in front of each of us. We can discover what's been ignored, expose what's been hidden, and change the atmosphere of our lives.

How we love today is primarily determined by how we were loved yesterday.

But how we will love tomorrow is directly correlated to how we choose to love today.

No matter what your love style has been, what it will be is completely up to you.

How Anxious Attachment Shows Up in Adulthood
1. Romantic Relationships

BEHAVIOR	EXPRESSION	UNDERLYING FEAR
Clinginess	Constant texting, frequent checking in	Fear of abandonment
Emotional highs and lows	Intense joy when close, despair when distant	Love feels unstable
Overinterpretation	Reading too much into messages or tone	Searching for signs of rejection
Difficulty trusting	Even in healthy relationships	Past wounds are projected forward
Conflict spirals	Escalation when feeling unseen	"If you loved me, you'd reassure me faster."

Insight: In love, they're looking for certainty in a world that once felt unpredictable. Their emotional volume is turned up in search of consistent safety.

2. Friendships

BEHAVIOR	EXPRESSION	UNDERLYING BELIEF
Feeling left out	Overthinking if not invited	"I'm not important to them."
Over-giving	Constantly checking in, doing favors	"If I'm useful, they won't leave."
Jealousy or comparison	Feeling threatened by other friendships	"I'm replaceable."

Insight: Anxious individuals often carry a relational radar, constantly scanning for signs of disconnection.

3. Parenting

BEHAVIOR	EXPRESSION	UNDERLYING FEAR
Seeking validation	Needing to be seen as a "good parent"	"I must earn my child's love."
Over-identification	Living through child's successes	"My worth is in being needed."
Struggling with separation	Difficulty allowing independence	Fear of emotional disconnection

Insight: In parenting, the anxious style can overcorrect for their own childhood neglect, creating enmeshment.

4. Work and Achievement

BEHAVIOR	EXPRESSION	UNDERLYING BELIEF
People-pleasing	Overcommitting, fear of saying no	"I'm only valuable if I perform."
Imposter syndrome	Doubting their abilities	"I'll be found out."
Sensitivity to criticism	Taking feedback personally	"I'm not enough."

Insight: In work, anxious attachment often seeks approval from authority figures to validate their worth.

5. Faith

BEHAVIOR	EXPRESSION	UNDERLYING FEAR
Performance-based spirituality	Over-serving, constant activity at church	"If I don't do enough, God will leave me."
Overemphasis on feelings	Equating God's presence with emotions	"If I don't feel Him, He's gone."
Spiritual comparison	Measuring worth by others' devotion	"Others are closer to God than me."
Frequent seeking of reassurance	Needing constant affirmation from pastors or community	"Am I really saved/loved?"

Insight: In faith, the anxious heart often chases certainty, trying to earn what God has already given—love and belonging.

How Avoidant Attachment Shows Up in Adulthood
1. Romantic Relationships

BEHAVIOR	EXPRESSION	UNDERLYING FEAR
Emotional distancing	Physically present, emotionally absent	Fear of engulfment
Shutting down	Silent treatment, withdrawal	Fear of emotional overload
Prioritizing space	Over-focus on work, hobbies, solitude	Fear of being needed too much
Minimizing intimacy	Downplaying the importance of relationship	Fear of losing self

Insight: Avoidant partners deeply desire love, but have been trained to believe it's dangerous. They protect themselves via emotional and physical distance.

2. Friendships

BEHAVIOR	EXPRESSION	UNDERLYING BELIEF
Surface-level closeness	Avoiding deep emotional sharing	"If I open up, I'll be judged."
Rarely asking for help	Managing everything alone	"Relying on others is risky."
Keeping emotions in	Stoic, neutral tone	"Feelings are irrelevant or unsafe."

Insight: Even close friendships can feel threatening when vulnerability is required. Individuals with avoidant tendencies may prefer structured or shared-activity friendships.

3. Parenting

BEHAVIOR	EXPRESSION	UNDERLYING FEAR
Low emotional engagement	Struggles with child's big feelings	"If I feel too much, I'll lose control."
Encouraging self-sufficiency too early	Avoids emotional dependency	"I don't know how to comfort."
Discomfort with physical affection	Minimal touch or praise	"Closeness is uncomfortable."

Insight: Avoidant parents may fear repeating what they experienced, and yet find themselves defaulting to the same behaviors.

5. Faith

BEHAVIOR	EXPRESSION	UNDERLYING FEAR
Intellectualizing faith	Preferring theology over intimacy with God	"Feelings about God aren't safe."
Keeping distance in prayer	Rarely expressing personal needs	"If I open up, I'll be disappointed."
Self-reliant spirituality	Emphasis on independence and discipline	"I can't depend on God or others."
Minimizing community	Viewing church as optional or secondary	"People can't be trusted with my soul."

Insight: In faith, avoidant hearts believe in God but struggle to receive His closeness, often substituting knowledge or discipline for intimacy.

How Disorganized Attachment Shows Up in Adulthood
1. Romantic Relationships

BEHAVIOR	EXPRESSION	UNDERLYING FEAR
Push-pull dynamics	Fluctuates between clinginess and distance	Fear of abandonment and engulfment
Emotional reactivity	Intense conflict, testing behaviors	Fear of rejection or betrayal
Self-sabotage	Ending or harming stable relationships	Fear of being seen and hurt
Hypervigilance	Constantly scanning for signs of betrayal	"People can't be trusted."

Insight: The disorganized partner is not manipulative; they are dysregulated. Their unpredictability is often a reenactment of childhood trauma.

2. Friendships

BEHAVIOR	EXPRESSION	UNDERLYING BELIEF
Inconsistency	Rapid changes in closeness and distance	"People leave once they see me."
Testing loyalty	Creating drama to assess trustworthiness	"If you stay after this, it's real."
Isolation after conflict	Ghosting or cutting people off	"I'd rather leave than be left."

Insight: Disorganized individuals often long for community but fear betrayal. Friendships can feel like emotional minefields.

3. Parenting

BEHAVIOR	EXPRESSION	UNDERLYING FEAR
Overwhelmed by child's emotion	Becomes anxious or shuts down	"I don't know how to soothe or stay calm."
Overcompensating	Tries too hard to be the opposite parent	Fear of becoming like their own parents
Inconsistent responses	Shifts between leniency and harshness	Lack of internal regulation

Insight: Disorganized parents often carry unresolved trauma. They may strive to protect their children while unconsciously passing on patterns of fear and confusion.

4. Work and Achievement

BEHAVIOR	EXPRESSION	UNDERLYING BELIEF
All-or-nothing effort	Burnout cycles followed by withdrawal	"I'm only worthy when over-performing."
Reactivity to authority	Struggles with feedback or structure	"I can't trust people in charge."
Fear of success or visibility	Sabotaging opportunities	"If I stand out, I'll get hurt."

Insight: At work, disorganized individuals often excel under pressure until their trauma gets triggered. Then, they may suddenly disengage or self-destruct.

5. Faith

BEHAVIOR	EXPRESSION	UNDERLYING FEAR
Push-pull with God	Intense devotion followed by withdrawal	"God will hurt me or leave me."
Distrust of leaders	Questioning motives, difficulty submitting	"Authority can't be safe."
Crisis-driven spirituality	Only seeking God when overwhelmed	"I can't count on steady love."
Self-sabotage in growth	Quitting when progress feels too vulnerable	"If I draw near, I'll be exposed."

Insight: In faith, disorganized hearts long for God yet fear Him deeply, often reenacting human betrayal and trauma in their relationship with Him.

FOOTNOTES

[1] Bowlby, John. *Attachment and Loss*
(Basic Books Classics, 1983)

[2] Main & Solomon (1986) introduced disorganized/
disoriented attachment based on incoherent or
contradictory behavior in the Strange Situation.

[3] Siegel, Daniel. *Personality and Wholeness in Therapy*
(New York: Norton, 2024), 19.

[4] Siegel, Daniel. *Attachment and Relational Resilience
Across the Lifespan* (mindsightinstitute.com, 2023)

[5] van der Kolk, Bessel. *The Body Keeps the Score*
(London: Penguin, 2015)

[6] Menanno, Julie. *Secure Love* (New York: Simon & Schuster), 63.

[7] Siegel, Daniel. *The Power of Showing Up* (New York: Ballentine Books, 2021)

[8] Siegel, Daniel. *Attachment Across the Life Span.*

[9] Ibid.

[10] Ibid.

[11] This constant scanning is part of what Porges calls "neuroception," our body's unconscious way of asking, "Am I safe right now?"

[12] Thompson, Curt. *The Soul of Shame.* (Donners Grove: Intervarsity Press, 2015)

[13] Ibid.

[14] Daniels, David. *The Enneagram, Relationships, and Intimacy* (New York: Morgan James Publishing, 2025), xxxvi.

[15] Siegel, *Attachment Across the Life Span.*

Also from Kevin A. Thompson...